NEWTON'S NOTEBOOK

Brenden I Hope this Book
Helps you on Your Journey to
a great Life. I Love you So
Much Son.

Love,
your Dad

NEWTON'S NOTEBOOK

The Life, Times, and Discoveries of
Sir Isaac Newton

Written and Compiled by
JOEL LEVY

Running Press
Philadelphia • London

Library of Congress Control Number:
2008944127

ISBN: 978-0-7624-3778-8

Conceived, designed, and produced by
Quid Publishing
Level 4, Sheridan House,
114 Western Road,
Hove,
BN3 1DD
England
www.quidpublishing.com

Design by: Lindsey Johns

Running Press Book Publishers
2300 Chestnut St.
Philadelphia, PA 19103-4371

Visit us on the web!
www.runningpress.com

Contents

Introduction

THE POPULAR IMAGE OF ISAAC
NEWTON IS OF A BRAINY
BOFFIN LOST IN THOUGHT
BENEATH A TREE UNTIL
LITERALLY STRUCK WITH A
BRIGHT IDEA, IN THE SHAPE OF
A FALLING APPLE. LIKE SO
MUCH ELSE CONCERNING THIS
COMPLEX AND EXTRAORDINARY
MAN, THIS STORY IS A LEGEND,
IF NOT A MYTH. NEWTON
HIMSELF NEVER MENTIONED
APPLES DIRECTLY IN HIS
ACCOUNT OF THE CONCEPTION
OF THE THEORY OF GRAVITY,
ALTHOUGH HE DID APPARENTLY
SUGGEST TO OTHERS THAT IT
WAS THROUGH THE CONTEM-
PLATION OF AN APPLE HANGING
FROM A TREE, ALONGSIDE
CONSIDERATION OF THE ORBIT
OF THE MOON, THAT HE FIRST
CONCEIVED OF A SINGLE
POWER OF ATTRACTION
AFFECTING BOTH OBJECTS.
THIS SCRAP OF ANECDOTE WAS
PASSED ON TO THOSE WHO
POPULARIZED HIS WORK AFTER
HIS DEATH, AND EVENTUALLY
TRANSFORMED INTO AN
ENDURING MYTH. IT IS AN APT
METAPHOR FOR THE STORY OF
NEWTON HIMSELF.

Even within his own lifetime the process of transformation had begun, as the mythical Newton shed the layers of his true identity—his troubled psychology, his pursuit of esoteric and occult wisdom, his religious heresies—to leave a hard, bright core: the ultimate scientist. In the centuries since, Newton has become the epitome of the scientist, the paragon of rational materialism, discarding speculation and supposition and holding only with what can be proved. Implacably, he cleared away the dead wood of eons of mysticism and supersti-tion to expose the shining truths beneath: laws of nature, the universe as a giant machine, all cogs and gears.

As with all myths and legends there is a kernel of truth to this tale. Newton's achievements were epochal and transforma-tive, his method radical and powerful. The approach he perfected, today known as the scientific method, has proved to be the most powerful tool in the history of human thought; wielding it, he made fantastic discoveries: calculus, the laws of motion, the theory of universal gravitation, the explanation of color and the rainbow, an entire system of the world, elegant, simple, and consonant to itself.

Return, however, to the story of Newton's apple. Even his own account was a convenient fiction. He did not arrive at the theory of gravity all at once while seated in his garden contem-plating an apple. In truth the process was lengthy and com-plex, stretching over years, occurring in fits and starts, owing its true inspiration to sources that few people know about. Newton was not a "scientist." The word did not exist; he accounted himself a "natural philosopher," a broad term that encompassed many areas of thought that today lie far outside the bounds of science. He was an alchemist, a student of the occult, mixing toxic metals in his laboratory in his search for the Philosopher's Stone. He was a Biblical archaeologist, exca-vating scripture for ancient wisdom. He was a prophet, obsessively interpreting the Book of Revelation in an attempt to pin down the Second Coming and the End of Days.

Newton's humanity has also been obscured. The majority of anecdotes about his life, par-ticularly his early years, were gathered by John Conduitt and William Stukeley, his nephew-in-law and friend. More importantly, they were acolytes, worshipers at the altar of Newton concerned to construct and perpetuate a sanitized, sanctified image of the great man. In so doing they obscured the often unpalatable truth. Newton was difficult, troubled, even tortured. He had a pathological hatred of dispute, pur-

Isaac Newton was an immensely complex man. Undoubtedly a scientific genius, whose incredible discoveries have illuminated the world, he also exhibited obsessions with alchemy, the occult, and the prediction of the Second Coming. What is more, Newton's personal life was a deeply troubled one.

sued vendettas and grudges, struggled with his sexuality, brooded over the trauma of his childhood abandonment, and flirted with madness.

To do justice to Newton in a confined space and at the same time attempt an account of his science has necessarily required some contraction and simplification. It seems appropriate to quote Newton himself: "I heartily beg that what I have here done may be read with candour; and that the defects in a subject so difficult be not so much reprehended as kindly supplied, and investigated by new endeavours of my readers."

A Note About Dates

In Newton's lifetime Britain still followed the old Julian calendar, and the switch to the Gregorian calendar was yet to come, so that the "Old Style" dates were 10–11 days behind the "New Style" Continental, modern ones, and the New Year only began on March 25. In accordance with normal practice, the years given here are in the New Style, so that although the date of Newton's death, March 20, was considered by the British at the time to be in the year 1726, the modern reckoning, given here, is that he died in 1727.

CHAPTER ONE

A FARMER'S SON

The Birth of Newton

IS GENIUS AN ACCIDENT OF BIRTH OR THE PRODUCT OF ITS TIME? NEWTON WAS BORN IN THE MIDST OF AN ERA OF GREAT CIVIL, RELIGIOUS, AND INTELLECTUAL TURMOIL THAT WOULD FOSTER AND SHAPE HIS ACHIEVEMENTS. YET THE CORNER OF ENGLAND WHERE HIS FAMILY LIVED WAS QUIET AND RELATIVELY PEACEFUL, AND HIS BACKGROUND AND IMMEDIATE FAMILY OFFERED NO HINT OF INCIPIENT GREATNESS.

Born in 1642 on Christmas Day—a date that would come to hold great significance, in his own mind at least—Isaac Newton was a posthumous child. His father, Isaac Newton Senior, had died in early October at the age of 36. His will recorded that he was "sick of body but of good and perfect memory," suggesting that he had been ill for some time.

The Newtons were a farming family from Lincolnshire, in the east of England, on the cusp between yeomanry and minor gentry, at a time when such socio-economic distinctions were still all-important, but becoming increasingly fluid. Isaac Newton's great-great-grandfather, John Newton of Westby, had

When Newton was to be knighted in 1705 he was required to prove his pedigree. As part of the process he drew up a family tree showing his paternal lineage, carefully including the descent of his already ennobled cousin, Sir John Newton. A simplified version is shown below.

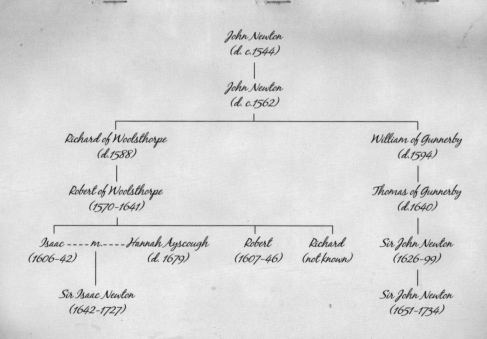

John Newton
(d. c.1544)

John Newton
(d. c.1562)

Richard of Woolsthorpe
(d. 1588)

Robert of Woolsthorpe
(1570–1641)

William of Gunnerby
(d. 1594)

Thomas of Gunnerby
(d. 1640)

Isaac - - - - m - - - - Hannah Ayscough
(1606–42)   (d. 1679)

Robert
(1607–46)

Richard
(not known)

Sir John Newton
(1626–99)

Sir Isaac Newton
(1642–1727)

Sir John Newton
(1651–1734)

transformed the family fortunes in the mid-16th century, bequeathing to his descendants an estate substantial enough for them to prosper. His grandfather, Robert, had purchased the manor of Woolsthorpe as the family home, and at birth the infant Isaac's fate would have seemed well mapped out—a prosperous farmer of sheep who would steward the family estate for the next generation.

But there was one vital difference between Isaac and his forefathers: his mother. Hannah Ayscough was the daughter of minor gentry, from a family in which the men were educated; Isaac's uncle William Ayscough was the rector of nearby Burton Coggles. Although the family tree he later drew up would, typically, ignore the distaff side, it was to the Ayscoughs that he owed his education, thus gaining the distinction of being the first of his line of Newtons to be able to sign his own name, and much else besides.

Newton's home county of Lincolnshire, situated in the east of England.

No Bigger than a Quart Pot

Newton was said to have been a tiny, sickly child, "so little they could put him in a quart pot." Two women brought in to help Hannah with the birth were sent for medicine, but such was the baby's frailty they assumed their mission to be futile, and, according to Newton's nephew John Conduitt, "sat down on a stile by the way & said there was no occasion for making haste for they were sure the child would be dead before they could get back."

"Sir I.N. told me that … when he was born he was so little they could put him into a quart pot & so weakly that he was forced to have a bolster all around his neck to keep it on his shoulders."

— JOHN CONDUITT, *LIFE OF NEWTON* (DRAFT)

Modern biographers regard such tales with skepticism, as part of the mythologizing of Newton that began even during his own lifetime; such stories helped to construct the narrative of a child of destiny. They may also have served to bolster Newton's own claim that he was born prematurely; a claim that may have been intended to obscure any suggestion that he might have been conceived out of wedlock, given that his parents were only married in April. It is true, however, that baby Isaac was not christened until January 1, 1643, suggesting that his life had indeed hung in the balance for a week.

Abandonment

ALMOST CERTAINLY THE FORMATIVE EXPERIENCE OF NEWTON'S CHILDHOOD WAS HIS SEPARATION FROM HIS MOTHER. AFTER THREE YEARS OF WHICH VERY LITTLE IS KNOWN, BUT DURING WHICH PERIOD HE HAD HIS MOTHER ALL TO HIMSELF, YOUNG ISAAC'S WORLD WAS TURNED UPSIDE DOWN BY HER REMARRIAGE. A CONDITION OF THE MARRIAGE CONTRACT WAS THAT HANNAH SHOULD GO TO LIVE WITH HER NEW HUSBAND, LEAVING THE INFANT BEHIND AT WOOLSTHORPE TO BE RAISED BY HIS MATERNAL GRANDPARENTS.

Newton may have been fatherless but he was well provided for. His father's will shows that the Woolsthorpe estate was worth over £450 and included 234 sheep and 46 head of cattle, at a time when the typical yeoman left little more than £100 and an average flock in the region consisted of fewer than 40 sheep. Hannah ruled this little empire from the manor house, a sturdy medieval building of gray limestone that lay at the center of a small hamlet of lesser buildings, just a short distance west of the Great North Road and a few miles south of the market town of Grantham.

Mr. and Mrs. Smith

Still only around 30, the widow Ayscough-Newton caught the eye of Barnabas Smith, rector of North Witham, a well-to-do man of 63 who had lost his previous wife just six months earlier. An Oxford graduate, Smith seems to have had pretensions to learning. He owned a large notebook (at a time when paper was extremely expensive), in which he made a few desultory attempts to copy out passages from his extensive library of over 200 mainly theological works. His stepson would inherit both notebook and library. The latter is credited with having begun a religious education that would lead him deep into heresy (see pages 70–1), while the former was put to good use as the birthplace of calculus and Newtonian mechanics. Newton called it the "Waste Book," perhaps indicating his opinion of Smith's academic efforts.

Barnabas and Hannah were married in early 1646 and she moved in with him; little Isaac was to stay behind at Woolsthorpe. Possibly her parents, who would raise the boy, devised the arrangement to help safeguard their interest in the Woolsthorpe estate. In the words of Richard Westfall, the pre-eminent

Newtonian mechanics took form in Newton's "Waste Book." The two axioms below would later form the basis of Newton's first law of motion, sometimes referred to as the law of inertia.

"1. If a quantity once move it will never rest unlesse hindered by some externall caus. 2. A quantity will always move on in the same streight line (not changing the determination nor celerity of its motion) unlesse some externall cause divert it."

Woolsthorpe

Woolsthorpe. Isaac Newton was born in a bedroom at the top of the stairs. The house was later adorned with sundials carved by Newton's own hand.

biographer of Newton, Smith proved to be "vigorous, not to say lusty" despite his advanced years, fathering three children with Hannah—Mary, Benjamin, and Hannah—before dying eight years later.

Lasting Damage

As an adult Newton was withdrawn, moody, intense, and prone to fits of rage and long-harbored grudges. Most biographers point to the trauma of separation from his mother as the root of many of these emotional issues. The few first-hand sources that survive from his early years give tantalizing glimpses of his psychology. As a young teenager Newton recorded lists of words in an exercise book now known as the Morgan Notebook (it is owned by the Pierpont Morgan Library), amongst them, under the heading "Kindred, & Titles," the following: " Brother. Bastard… Benjamite… Father. Fornicator…" ("Benjamite" can be taken to mean "one who favors the youngest son.")

Even more alarming are some of the sins Newton noted in what is now known as the Fitzwilliam Notebook, written in 1662 when he was an undergraduate. By this time Smith was long dead, but Newton clearly still brooded over the bitterness of his childhood years. Among amusingly trivial transgressions, such as "Making pies on a Sunday night," comes the startling admission that he threatened arson against his mother and stepfather.

TO THE MANOR BORN
Isaac's great-great-grand-father John Newton of Westby purchased an estate at Woolsthorpe for his son Richard. It passed to Isaac's grandfather Robert, who in 1623 added to it by buying the manor house in which Isaac was later born.

A World at War

WOOLSTHORPE LAY JUST A FEW HUNDRED YARDS TO THE WEST OF THE GREAT NORTH ROAD, THE THOROUGHFARE FOR ARMIES MARCHING UP AND DOWN THE COUNTRY, YET THE INFANT NEWTON'S DIRECT EXPERIENCE OF THE ENGLISH CIVIL WAR—OR THE GREAT REBELLION AS IT HAS ALSO BEEN KNOWN—WAS PROBABLY LIMITED. ITS IMPACT ON HIS WORLD, HOWEVER, WOULD BE LASTING AND SIGNIFICANT.

The Great Rebellion was ostensibly a battle between Parliament and the king—between those who believed that sovereignty ultimately rested in the person of the monarch, and those who believed that it rested in Parliament, and that the king ruled only with Parliament's consent and by extension that of his people. In practice there was a great deal more to it than this. It was also a battle over religion, which at times threatened to turn the country into a hotbed of fanaticism, but which also opened the door for a variety of dissenting approaches to Christianity, different from the prevailing orthodoxy. In this sense it was also a rebellion of the mind; perhaps a necessary precondition for the Scientific Revolution that Newton would usher in.

Cavalier or Roundhead?

His stepfather and his uncle were clergymen at a time when such men were losing their livelihoods and their lives over matters of conscience, but both Barnabas Smith and William Ayscough appear to have made an accommodation with the new political and religious order. This has not prevented many Newton biographers from assuming that the Newtons, as minor gentry with a vested interest in maintaining the status quo, were royalist sympathizers. But Newton's virulent anti-Catholic bias in later life suggests a background of staunch Protestantism, which might have set his family at odds with the king.

In practice such matters were of little concern, for Isaac's childhood was largely untroubled by the war, despite the momentous events that took place during his infancy. The year of Newton's birth had seen the beginning of the Civil War proper. In January the king had fled London, and the first pitched battle of the war, at Edgehill, had taken place in October. In May 1643 there was a skirmish near Grantham and, although there were other minor flare-ups nearby over the next decade, Lincolnshire was quickly secured for the Parliamentary side. Soldiers may have passed through the fields of the Newton estate, foraged nearby, and even have been billeted at Woolsthorpe, but there is no record of any such occurrence.

Above: King Charles I in regal mode. It was his insistence on the divine right of kings that caused the breach with Parliament and triggered the English Civil War.

Right: The arms of the republican Commonwealth of England, which ruled from 1649 to 1660. The motto *Pax quæritur bello* means "Peace is sought through war."

"And if 'twere possible our fathers old
 Should live againe, and tread upon this mould,
 And see all things confused, overthrowne,
 They would not know this Countrey for their own.
 For England hath no likelihood or show
 Of what it was but seventy years ago;
 Religion, manners, life, and shapes of men,
 Are much unlike the people that were then"

— From the pamphlet, *The World Turned Upside Down*, 1647

In 1649 Charles I was executed and England soon passed into the control of Cromwell. For ten years the former kingdom became a commonwealth and then a protectorate, which in turn fell apart after Cromwell's death. In 1660 Charles II was restored to the throne. Yet none of this seems to have had much impact on Newton's life, restricted to a tiny area of Lincolnshire. By the time he emerged onto a larger stage, as an undergraduate at Cambridge, the turmoil of the Civil War was over. But its themes lingered on, becoming important influences on his thinking. The unorthodox approach to religion would find expression in Newton's unorthodoxy. The conflict with a pro-Catholic king would be mirrored in Newton's dispute with King James II. Civil strife had swept new men into important positions at the universities, and Newton would be the beneficiary of their new ways of thinking.

The trial of King Charles. Many years later, Isaac would clash with Charles's son, James, in a legal battle of his own (see pages 110–11).

School Days

THE OBVIOUS PLACE TO LOOK FOR THE ROOTS OF SOME OF THE GREATEST INTELLECTUAL ACCOMPLISHMENTS IN HISTORY IS IN NEWTON'S EARLY SCHOOLING, BUT THE EVIDENCE ABOUT THIS PERIOD IS CONTRADICTORY. HIS FORMAL EDUCATION WAS CONSTRAINED BY THE LIMITS OF THE CURRICULUM AND INITIALLY HE PROVED AN UNDISTINGUISHED SCHOLAR, BUT ANECDOTES AND HIS ADOLESCENT SCRIBBLINGS REVEAL THE FIRST STIRRINGS OF A PRECOCIOUS INTELLECT.

In August 1653 Barnabas Smith died and Newton's mother came back to Woolsthorpe, with his three half-siblings in tow. Whether this was a joyous or bitter reunion is a matter for conjecture, but looking at Newton's later list of pre-Whitsunday 1662 sins, most biographers tend to think the latter: the psychological damage had already been done.

Little evidence survives of the next year and a half, although it is known that young Isaac attended day schools in the neighborhood, and possibly enjoyed a fractious relationship with his siblings; "Punching my sister" is number 24 on his list of sins. Possibly it was a relief when, in 1655, he turned 12 and was old enough to go to grammar school in Grantham. The town was seven miles (11 kilometers) away from Woolsthorpe, too far to commute each day, necessitating that he board there. So began his education proper.

The King's School

The Free Grammar School of Edward VI (also known as the King's School) had been established on the site of an older school, by charter, in the mid-16th century. By the time of Newton's attendance notable alumni already included William Cecil, chief minister of Elizabeth I, and the philosopher Henry More, who would come to be a major influence on Newton, as would the headmaster, Henry Stokes, a Cambridge man.

The school consisted of a single room housing around 80 pupils. Newton was initially placed in the lowest set and sat at the back (students were ranked, and seated, by performance). A solitary and unsociable child, he probably struggled to fit in. Anecdotes survive that he was "a sober, silent, thinking lad" who "never was known scarce to play with the boys abroad."

Taken from a letter Newton copied into his notebook, presumably to a school or college friend.

Loving ffreind
It is commonly reported that you are sick.
Truly I am sorry for that. But I am much more sorry that you got your sicknesse (for that they say too) by drinking too much. I ernestly desire you first to repent of your haveing beene drunk & then to seeke to recover your health. And if it pleas God that you ever bee well againe then have a care to live healthfully & soberly for time to come. This will bee very well pleasing to all your freinds & especially to
Your very loving freind
I. N.

Before Whitsunday 1662.

Using the word (God) openly   1

Eating an apple at Thy house   2

Making a feather while on Thy day   3

Denying that I made it.   4

Making a mousetrap on Thy day   5

Contriving of the chimes on Thy day   6

Squirting water on Thy day   7

Making pies on Sunday night   8

Swimming in a kimnel on Thy day   9

Putting a pin in Iohn Keys hat on Thy day to prick him.   10

Carelessly hearing and committing many sermons   11

Refusing to go to the close at my mothers command.   12

Threatning my father and mother Smith to burne them and the house over them   13

Wishing death and hoping it to some   14

Striking many   15

Having uncleane thoughts words and actions and dreamese.   16

Stealing cherry cobs from Eduard Storer   17

Denying that I did so   18

Denying a crossbow to my mother and grandmother though I knew of it   19

Setting my heart on money learning pleasure more than Thee   20

A relapse   21

A relapse   22

A breaking again of my covenant renued in the Lords Supper.   23

Punching my sister   24

Even after a few years he was not well liked. Stukeley recounts that he cared not for the "trifling sports" of his schoolfellows, but tried to "teach them … to play philosophically." Here can be read evidence of a boy set apart by his intellect, yet without the social or emotional intelligence to make friends; evidence that could be an indication that Newton suffered from some form of Asperger's Syndrome. He could also be something of a prig, as evidenced by a sanctimonious letter he composed to a "Loving ffriend" as an older teenager (see opposite).

Latin and more Latin

His initial slow progress probably also owes much to the nature of the curriculum taught at the time, where facility with Latin was assumed to be the path not simply to learning but to virtue. Accordingly, Newton was taught Latin, Latin, and more Latin, with a little Greek and Hebrew thrown in. Astonishingly, given the accomplishments he would achieve just a few months after leaving school, he received little training in mathematics beyond practical arithmetic for future farmers. But like many prodigies, he was an autodidact, supplementing and extending his restricted schooling with wide reading, initially of the books he had inherited from his stepfather, and later in the library of St. Wulfram's church in Grantham. It was filled with theological tracts to which he was directed by one of his teachers, a Puritan named John Angell. This early exposure to a mass of religious material helped to shape the profound convictions he held for the rest of his life.

Newton's list of the sins he had committed before Whitsun 1662, mainly detailing his run-ins with members of his family and petty violations of the Fourth Commandment (refraining from work on the Sabbath—"Thy Day").

"a sober, silent, thinking lad"

Scientific Inspirations

THOUGH HE WAS TAUGHT NOTHING AT SCHOOL THAT WAS REMOTELY SIMILAR TO WHAT WE WOULD CALL SCIENCE, NEWTON NEVERTHELESS BEGAN HIS EDUCATION IN ASPECTS OF NATURAL PHILOSOPHY. HE HAD A TASTE AND A TALENT FOR MAKING THINGS, MIXING REMEDIES, PIGMENTS, AND POTIONS, DRAWING AND SCRATCHING; ALL TYPICAL SCHOOLBOY PURSUITS, BUT IN HIS PRACTICE OF THEM IT IS POSSIBLE TO DISCERN THE FIRST STIRRINGS OF HIS PRECOCIOUS GIFTS.

William Stukeley would later collect anecdotes of how Newton had filled the walls of his room with drawings: charcoal sketches of plants, birds and beasts, men and ships, portraits of the dead king, of John Donne, and of his schoolmaster Stokes. But there were also more abstract figures: lines, triangles, and circles. These would seem to be significant markers for his future, although D.T. Whiteside, the pre-eminent scholar of Newton's mathematics, has suggested that, "It would need the blindness of maternal love to read into these … burgeoning … mathematical precocity."

What skill in drawing he did possess may have been developed in part by following the instructions divulged in one of his favorite books, one that seems to have played a major part in setting him on the road to becoming a scientist. That book was John Bate's 1634 *Mysteries of Nature and Art*, a rambling and unsystematic collection of secrets, wonders, recipes, and folklore. It consisted of four parts, "The first of water workes. The second of Fyer workes, The third of Drawing,

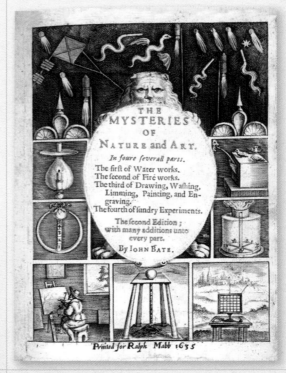

The frontispiece of John Bate's *Mysteries of Nature and Art*, the book credited with introducing Newton to the joys of natural philosophy, and, with its section detailing "Sundry Experiments," inspiring him to start investigating the natural world.

OF DRAWING WITH THE PEN

Let the thing which you intend to draw stand before you, so that the light be not hindred from falling upon it. & with a pointed peice of charecole draw it rudely & lightly when you have don see if it be well don; if not wipe out with your wing & begin agine, & so draw it till it bee well. yn wipe it over gently with your wing, so that you may perceive your former strokes; yn with your black chalk or pensill draw it perfectly & curiously as you can, & shaddow it as the light falleth upon it. If you draw on blew paper when you have finished your draught wet your paper in fair wait & let it dry of it self. & so the drawing will hold fast on.

— INSTRUCTIONS ON HOW TO DRAW, COPIED BY NEWTON FROM BATE'S *MYSTERIES OF NATURE AND ART*

Coloring, Painting, and Engraving, The fourth of divers Experiments, as wel serviceable as delightful." Newton discovered it when he was about 13 and copied out many passages into his notebook.

This wonderful book would spark or stoke in him a fascination with models and machines, sundials and stargazing, colors and light, chemicals and potions, prefiguring many of the obsessions and discoveries of his later life. Yet it was almost entirely practical in bent: it described to the reader things to do and make, with few concessions to theories or systems of the world.

First Leaps in Experimentation

Perhaps inspired by Bate's "delightful Experiments," Newton performed one of his own; he would later tell the Earl of Pembroke that it was the first he ever made. It was on September 3, 1658, the day of Oliver Cromwell's death, when a great storm battered the land with high winds. To estimate the strength of the storm, Newton leaped into the air, first with the wind and then against it. He noted the distances between takeoff and landing, and compared them to similar leaps he had made on a calm day; in this way he was able to measure what he called "the vis [force] of the storm" and inform his schoolmates that the wind was a foot stronger than any he had previously experienced. In a different version of the story Newton used the insight gleaned from his little experiment to win a jumping contest.

Early Notebooks

NEWTON'S ENTHUSIASM FOR BATE'S *MYSTERIES OF NATURE AND ART*, HIS INTEREST IN RECIPES AND DEVICES, AND EVEN SMALL CLUES TO HIS OTHERWISE HIDDEN PSYCHOLOGY, ARE KNOWN THANKS TO THE SURVIVAL OF A COUPLE OF HIS EARLY NOTEBOOKS. THOUGH LITTLE TO GO ON IN BUILDING A PICTURE OF THE FORMATIVE YEARS OF HIS LIFE, THESE PRECIOUS SOURCES, PRIMARILY THE MORGAN NOTEBOOK, OFFER A UNIQUE AND VALUABLE WINDOW INTO NEWTON'S ADOLESCENT MIND.

One of Newton's strengths as a thinker and worker was his meticulous and systematic approach, which has also had the advantage of leaving a trail, albeit scant at times, of compelling evidence of his thought processes. Westfall describes this as "his desire, perhaps even compulsion, to organise and categorise information." From early in his life he would write things down to help himself digest and assimilate information, state clearly problems, and begin to work toward answers, and he would do this in "pocketbooks"—notebooks made from sheets of paper sewn together and bound in vellum.

One of the earliest surviving notebooks, known as the Latin Exercise Book, reveals a few pathetic lines, written as Latin practice, which hint at his alienation, loneliness, and despair around the time he was starting at school (see quote). Later, probably around 1659, he spent 2½ pence given to him by his mother on a small exercise book, on the flyleaf of which he inscribed the phrase "Isacus Newton hunc librum possidet"; effectively, "this book belongs to Isaac Newton." (It is a notable peculiarity of Newton during his school days that he seems to have felt the urge to leave traces of his identity, carving his signature onto wood and stonework in his rooms, on the desks at school, and even on the windowsills.)

Into this exercise book, which is now known as the Morgan Notebook, Newton copied out long passages from Bate in tiny, careful handwriting, with characters sometimes just a few millimeters high. Later he started from the other end of the notebook and copied out lists of words from Francis Gregory's *Nomenclatura brevis anglo-latino*, adding some telltale ones of his own (see page 13). The central pages he later used for astronomical tables and an ecclesiastical calendar beginning in 1662, as well as a description of how to make a sundial.

"A little fellow; My poore helpe; Hee is paile; There is no room for me to sit; In the top of the house - In the Bottom of hell; What imployment is he fit for?; What is hee god for?... I will make an end. I cannot but weepe. I know not what to doe."

— NOTES FROM NEWTON'S LATIN EXERCISE BOOK, PROBABLY SOON AFTER STARTING SCHOOL.

Light my Fire

For all his diligence with extra-curricular material such as Bate, Newton was undistinguished in the classroom, at least until the fire of his competitive spirit was lit by a run-in with a bully. On the way to school one morning, a boy who ranked above him in class—possibly Arthur Storer, one of the boys with whom Newton was rooming (see page 24)—kicked him in the belly. Much later his nephew-in-law, John Conduitt, recorded Newton's reaction:

"he challenged the boy to fight, & they went out together into the Church yard... Tho Sir Isaac was not so lusty as his antagonist he had so much more spirit and resolution that he beat him till he declared he would fight no more ... & accordingly Sir Isaac pulled him along by the ears & thrust his face against the side of the Church."

Not content with besting the bully physically, Newton determined to crush him academically. Once his powerful intellect was engaged in schoolwork he quickly rose to the head of the class. It is difficult not to see this vignette as setting a pattern that would apply for the rest of his life, foreshadowing his bitter, drawn-out, and obsessive attempts to dominate and humble any who dared to challenge him.

Along with instructions on exactly how to mark out a sundial, Newton copied into the Morgan notebook diagrams from Bate. His crudely sketched lines, curves, and angles, labeled with letters, anticipate similar constructions that would later fill the pages of the *Principia*.

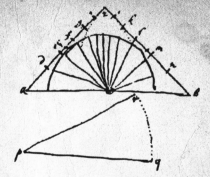

The use of the table on a Ruler whereby to make a dyall for any latitude.

Make a streight line which you intend shall stand for 6 a clock at the Morning & night let the line be as long as from the begining of the line of latitudes where there is a peice a bras to the degree of lattitude for which the Dyal is erected suppose the 50th degree & you make the line (a b) yn take the length of the line of the line of cords from the begining to the 60th degree set one foot of the compasses on a & make a scrow at t with the other foote. & doe the like at the point at b. yn draw two streight lines from the place where the two scrows meet at c to a & b. as (a c, a b) & marke those lines out according to the howerline on the ruler. as d e f g h i k l m n. Then take the point twixt a & b & make a circle & draw line from each of the former marke through the circle

to the center o. & those are the hower lines For the gnomen make a line as long as a c or b c was & that line must be joyned ro the dial suppose it b p. q. describe a circle as q. r. Then one point of the compasses on the line of cords at the begining & let the other foot reach to the figure which is the same with the lattitude supose 50. Then set one foote of the compasses upon g another on the circle suppose it reach to r yn draw a line from r to p. & that line is the line that casts the shaddow. &c

Models and Sundials

TOWARDS THE END OF HIS LIFE, NEWTON'S ACOLYTES COLLECTED TALES OF HIS CHILDHOOD. AMONG THE MOST STRIKING AND WHIMSICAL ARE THOSE WHICH TELL OF HIS DELIGHT IN CONSTRUCTING INGENIOUS DEVICES: WATERWHEELS, LANTERNS, AND SUNDIALS. THE SKILL AT HANDLING TOOLS THAT HE DEVELOPED WOULD STAND HIM IN GOOD STEAD WHEN HE LATER CAME TO CONSTRUCT INSTRUMENTS FOR HIS SCIENTIFIC RESEARCHES, MOST FAMOUSLY THE FIRST REFLECTING TELESCOPE.

When Stukeley came to Grantham in the 1720s, looking for anecdotes of Newton's youth, the people there remembered most "his strange inventions and extraordinary inclination for mechanical works." He made these "works" with tools, spending all of his pocket money on them until they filled his room.

Mills and Millers

He put the tools to use making cunningly crafted dolls' house furniture for the female playmates he preferred over male company. He was also inspired by the impressive new windmill recently constructed to the north of Grantham, and built a working copy (with help from instructions in Bate), with sails that spun when he put it on the roof. He even equipped the model with a treadmill into which he placed a mouse, which he encouraged to run by tugging its tail with a string or dangling a piece of corn in front of it, joking that the creature was his "miller." He made a four-wheeled cart driven by a crankshaft, which he could turn while he sat in the cart, thus powering himself along. He crafted a lantern out of "crimpled paper" and used it to light his way to school in winter, folding it up and storing it in his pocket during the day. When he attached it to the string of a kite and sent it aloft it "wonderfully affrighted all the neighbouring inhabitants for some time, and caus'd not a little discourse on market days, among the country people, when over their mugs of ale."

Indeed, Newton was so enthusiastic about making things that, pious as he was, he was unable to leave off this occupation even on Sundays. His list of 1662 confesses to such monstrous sins as "Making a mousetrap on Thy day," "Contriving of the chimes on Thy day," and "Twisting a cord on Sunday morning."

Newton's drawings of gravitationally and magnetically powered perpetual-motion machines (the former "may bee made one of two ways," he wrote). Although they date to later in his life, they well illustrate his enthusiasm for devices.

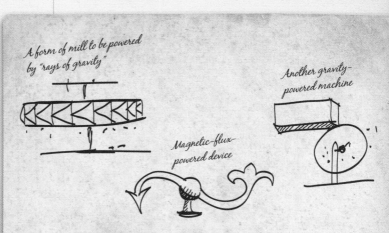

A form of mill to be powered by "rays of gravity"

Magnetic-flux powered device

Another gravity-powered machine

The sundial that Newton was said to have carved into a stone block in the walls of Woolsthorpe Manor with a penknife, and which was later cut out and presented to the Royal Society, where it is proudly displayed to this day.

"He showd another method of indulging his curiosity to find out the sun's motion, by making dyals of divers forms and constructions every where about the house, in his own chamber, in the entrys and rooms where ever the sun came."

— Stukeley, *Memoirs of Sir Isaac Newton's Life*, 1752

"Dyals of Divers Forms"

Even before starting at school in Grantham, Newton had become fascinated by the motion of the Sun across the heavens, and the ways in which its progress, and thus the time, could be measured. Stukeley records that he made "dyals of divers forms" with which he filled his own room, other rooms, and the entrance hall to his lodgings. A sundial mounted in a church near Woolsthorpe was supposedly cut by Newton at age nine, while in the possession of the Royal Society is a block cut from the walls of Woolsthorpe Manor, onto which he had carved a dial. Earlier, cruder ones were left behind; as he grew in height so they mounted the walls.

Young Newton marked out the hours, half-hours, and even quarter-hours with pegs driven into the stonework. He ran strings between them, upon which were mounted balls that could move back and forth, allowing him to mark out how the shadows changed with the seasons, and collated the results to give a sort of almanac.

In doing so he was internalizing connections: between time and space, between the motions of heavenly bodies and the geometry of lines, circles, arcs, and angles.

Apothecary's Apprentice

WHILE HE WAS AT SCHOOL IN GRANTHAM, NEWTON NEEDED A PLACE TO STAY. HE LODGED WITH THE FAMILY OF CLARK, THE APOTHECARY, WHO HAD AN ASSOCIATION WITH THE SCHOOL AND ROUTINELY BOARDED PUPILS AT HIS HOUSE ON THE HIGH STREET NEXT TO THE GEORGE INN. IT WAS HERE THAT HE FILLED HIS ROOM WITH DRAWINGS AND CLUTTERED UP THE HALLWAY WITH SUNDIALS, AND IT WAS HERE THAT HE SUPPOSEDLY HAD HIS FIRST AND ONLY BRUSH WITH HETEROSEXUAL ROMANCE.

Newton and the Clark family—consisting of John the apothecary, his wife, and her three children from a previous marriage: Catherine, Edward, and Arthur Storer—lived in rooms above the apothecary shop. It was probably crowded, and one of the lines from Newton's Latin Exercise Book—"In the top of the house – In the Bottom of Hell"—rather suggests that he was extremely unhappy, at least to begin with.

His relationship with the two boys was initially fraught. His 1662 list of sins included "Stealing cherry cobs from Eduard Storer" and "Denying that I did so," and "Peevishness at Master Clarks for a piece of bread and butter." Arthur is widely assumed to have been the bully who kicked him in the stomach, and who received a beating from Newton in return. Presumably he did not enjoy Newton's ongoing quest to humiliate him academically. Yet the three boys must have forged some lasting bonds of fellowship, for in later life Arthur Storer would relay to Newton observations of a comet all the way from Maryland in the New World, while Edward would be his tenant at Woolsthorpe Manor.

The Girl Next Door

Newton got on much better with Catherine. He preferred to play with her and her friends than with his schoolmates, delighting them with the dolls' house furniture he crafted. As they grew older a youthful romance supposedly bloomed between them. Stukeley recorded the tale thus:

"Sir Isaac and she being thus brought up together, it is said that he entertained a love for her, nor does she deny it. But her portion being not considerable, and he being [a] fellow of a college, it was incompatible with his fortunes to marry, perhaps his studies too."

Many biographers, however, regard this as little more than wishful thinking on the part of Catherine Storer, interviewed late in life when Newton had become a great man.

A Salve for all sores.

• • •

Take a pound of sheeps tallow a pound of turpentine & a pound of Virgin wax, a pint of sallet oyle, a quarter of a pound of Rosin: take also of Bugle, Smalsach, & plantaine halfe the quantity of the other or so much as will make a pinte boyle all these together on a soft fire of coles, always stir it till a 3d part be consumed, yn tak it from the fire & straine it through a new canvas cloth, into an earthen pot.

Recipes from Bate copied by Newton into his notebook.

Potions and Lotions

The most important consequence of Newton's stay with the Clarks appears to have been intellectual not social. Clark was a liberal thinker for his time, interested in learning but especially in the practical arts of his trade. He encouraged young Isaac to help him in the shop and to learn about the chemistry of mixing potions, salves, and medicines. The shop would have been an Aladdin's cave of exotic substances in jars, bottles, and packets— herbal extracts, minerals, and a colorful panoply of chemicals rich in the power to kill or cure, with names like calomel, ceruse, litharge, and white arsenic (salts of mercury, lead, and arsenic). Newton's copious transcription of recipes from Bate is testament to his fascination with the processes of mixing and preparing.

The chemistry Newton learned from Clark and Bate was a far cry from the science practiced in laboratories today. It was also very different from the alchemy that would later become Newton's primary obsession. But it introduced him to a world of chemicals, and to the craft of handling and mixing them. His later achievements in science would owe much to his ability to meld theory with practice, to think about and work with real-world phenomena as well as abstracts, to experiment and hypothesize.

> ## To make his powder to purge the head.
> ...
> Take ginger of the best, Orris powder of each halfe a dram; Pellitory of Spaine, & white Hellebore, of each halfe a dram; All these into a fine powder & searce them well & add to them two dropps of oyle of Anniseeds. And when you will use it take the quantitie of a barly corne & snuff it upp into your nose & it will cause a snezing, wherby it purgeth the head from all superfluous humours strengtheneth the memory causeth a cleare sight & is good for the thiknesse of hearing taken as abovesaid every other morning"

Apothecary jars and jugs containing the ingredients for remedies would have filled the shelves of Clark's apothecary shop. Many ingredients were sensitive to light and had to be stored in opaque porcelain jars.

"… exotic substances in jars, bottles, and packets — herbal extracts, minerals, and a colourful panoply of chemicals rich in the power to kill or cure …"

Fit for Nothing but the 'Versity

A TURNING POINT IN ISAAC NEWTON'S LIFE CAME IN LATE 1658, WHEN HIS MOTHER SUMMONED THE 17-YEAR-OLD HOME TO TAKE UP HIS FATHER'S MANTLE AS A GENTLEMAN FARMER. SENDING HIM TO SCHOOL HAD PROBABLY BEEN THE IDEA OF HER CAMBRIDGE-EDUCATED BROTHER WILLIAM, BUT NOW THE BOY HAD ACQUIRED MORE EDUCATION THAN HE NEEDED IT WAS TIME FOR HIM TO BEAR HIS RESPONSIBILITIES. BUT ISAAC HIMSELF HAD OTHER IDEAS, AND HE WAS SUPPORTED BY TWO IMPORTANT MENTORS.

Isaac and the life of a farmer were not well suited. By now his intellectual horizons had expanded and his massive faculties were fully engaged in the pursuit of learning; the everyday cares and concerns of running a working farm—what Conduitt would later call "low employments"—did not interest him. Tales abound of his absentmindedness, carelessness, and general lack of fitness for the role.

Daydream Believer

Sent to market with a servant, he would bribe the man to drop him off around the corner so that he could spend the day reading or constructing models. If forced to go to Grantham he would go to his old rooms at the Clarks and read a library of new books the apothecary had recently inherited from his schoolmaster brother. On the way home, forced by the steepness of Spittlegate hill to dismount and lead his horse, he would get so lost in thought that he would forget to remount and ended up leading the nag all the way home. According to one legend the horse actually slipped its bridle and trotted off, but the dreaming teenager failed to notice and walked on, bridle still in hand.

When set to watch sheep he wandered off and built little working waterwheels in the streams, with proper dams and sluices. Records of the manor court of Colsterworth indicate that on October 28, 1659, Newton was fined by "for suffering his sheep to break the stubbs ... for suffering his swine to trespass in the corn fields ... [and] for suffering his fence ... to be out of repair."

"(The servants) rejoic'd at parting with him, declaring, he was fit for nothing but the 'Versity." — STUKELEY, MEMOIRS

The Lion Cannot Deny His Mane

These antics did not go down well at home. His 1662 list of sins suggests unhappy consequences, including: "Refusing to go to the close at my mother's command," "Peevishness with my mother," "Falling out with the servants," "Calling Derothy Rose a jade." It was apparent to most that another path was marked out for him, or as Westfall puts it, "he had no more been able to deny his nature … than a lion can give up his mane."

At the King's School it is likely that Stokes had long been grooming his finest pupil for entrance to university. He argued with Hannah Smith that it was a waste of talent to keep Isaac from pursuing an academic route, and an effort that was bound to fail. He offered to let the boy stay at his own house (which rather suggests that Newton had outstayed his welcome with the Clarks), and to let her off the fees normally charged non-residents of Grantham. What is more, Hannah's brother, the Reverend William Ayscough, also brought his influence to bear.

Their combined efforts bore fruit, and in the autumn of 1660 Newton was allowed to return to school in Grantham to prepare for entry to Cambridge University. Stukeley recorded that the servants at Woolsthorpe, evidently exasperated by Newton's odd mixture of hostility, anger, lack of attentiveness, and apparent laziness, celebrated his departure (see quote opposite).

Returned to the classroom, Newton reached new heights of academic achievement. When it was time for him to leave, Stokes supposedly made him stand in front of the school while he sang his praises with tears in his eyes. In June 1661 he journeyed south to Cambridge to be admitted to Trinity, the greatest of the Cambridge colleges and the one his uncle had attended. So began perhaps the greatest undergraduate career of all time.

The crest of the King's School in Grantham. Newton supposedly carved his name into the wall of what is now the school library.

HONI SOIT QUI MAL Y PENSE

(Evil be to him who evil thinks)

CHAPTER TWO

NEWTON

AT

UNIVERSITY

Cambridge in the 1660s

IN GOING UP TO CAMBRIDGE, NEWTON ENTERED A WORLD APART, A COMMUNITY OF RELATIVELY SMALL SIZE BUT DISPROPORTIONATE INFLUENCE ON THE CIVIC, RELIGIOUS, AND INTELLECTUAL LIFE OF THE COUNTRY. YET CAMBRIDGE WAS NO ACADEMIC PARADISE OF DREAMING SPIRES AND EARNEST DEBATE; IT WAS DIRTY, ROWDY, AND OVER-CROWDED, RIVEN WITH POLITICAL TENSIONS AT EVERY LEVEL—A DANGEROUS PLACE FOR A NAÏVE YOUNG MAN FROM THE COUNTRY.

Cambridge in the 1660s was a small city situated at the crossing of important trade routes: the Great North Road and the waterways of the Fens to the east. Only 50 miles (80 kilometers) from London, it was tiny in comparison; a hundredth the size of the capital. Rows of cramped buildings pressed together over narrow streets, crowded with an insalubrious brew of residents. To strangers from grander places it must have presented a sorry prospect, and even 50 years later German traveler Zacharius von Uffenbach would declare it "no better than a village ... one of the sorriest places in the world." Yet to Newton, a country boy who had never traveled far from his home, it must have seemed like Babylon. The population of around 7000 people included about 3000 university men (students, graduates, and staff) along with a sizeable number of prostitutes and innkeepers to service their extra-curricular needs, and thieves and rogues to relieve them of any money they had left over. Indeed Cambridge was notoriously dangerous for students.

Town vs. Gown

Some of the threat of violence derived from tensions between town and gown; that is, between the ordinary townspeople and the institution that dominated them. Not only did the university account for a sizeable chunk of the population and economy of the city, it also held most of the political and legal authority, and resentment toward wealthy and arrogant students and academics was compounded by the autocratic manner in which the university authorities ran affairs. The vice-chancellor, the man who ran the university, was effectively the feudal overlord of Cambridge. Although a Royal Charter of 1600 had granted the city civic authorities of its own, including a mayor, it ended with a clause stipulating: "Nothing in this charter shall prejudice or impede the privileges, liberties and profits of the Chancellor, Masters and Scholars of the University."

The Famousest College

The exceptions to the city's unsavory aspect were the colleges, imposing buildings along the River Cam. Most impressive of them all was the College of the Holy and Undivided Trinity, founded by Henry VIII in 1546. A contemporary of Newton's described it as "the famousest College in the University." Intellectually the college dominated the university; it had the most important professors and produced the most important graduates.

Cambridge, a market town located at the edge of fenland where major trade routes cross.

Trinity College in the University of Cambridge

Following the Restoration of Charles II in 1660, Trinity was a flourishing community of more than 400 men, including fellows, scholars, clerks, choristers, servants, and almsmen. Newton had gained access thanks to his uncle William, and Humphrey Babington, brother of Mrs. Clark the apothecary's wife and himself a fellow of Trinity. According to Stukeley, Babington "is said to have had a particular kindness for him, which probably was owing to his own ingenuity." He would become an important influence on Newton's career.

"... most of [the streets are] so very narrow that should two wheelbarrows meet in the largest of their thoroughfares they are enough to make a stop for half an hour before they can well clear themselves of one another to make room for passengers. The buildings in many parts of the town are so little and so low that they looked more like huts for pygmies than houses for men."

— AN ANONYMOUS 17TH-CENTURY VISITOR TO CAMBRIDGE

View of Trinity College in the 17th century, facing west. Newton lived in rooms on the north side and later to the right of the great gate.

SLAPDOWN
The vice-chancellor was not shy of using his powers. The year before Newton's arrival, for instance, the mayor, Edward Chapman, had been humiliated in a run-in with the university authorities, after daring to release from the Tolbooth Gaol three men who had been committed there by Vice-Chancellor Dr. Ferne. He was forced to apologize in a letter: "I hereby acknowledge the error and do promise not to do or to my power suffer anything hereafter to be done that may anyways infringe the liberties or privileges of this University to my knowledge."

A Solitary and Dejected Scholar

NEWTON WAS HARDLY EQUIPPED WITH THE SOCIAL SKILLS NEEDED TO BECOME A POPULAR MAN ABOUT TOWN, AND HIS SITUATION WAS MADE MUCH WORSE BY THE LOWLY POSITION HE WAS FORCED TO ADOPT IN THE UNIVERSITY'S STRICT SOCIO-ECONOMIC HIERARCHY. IN TERMS OF THE HISTORICAL RECORD NEWTON WAS MORE OR LESS INVISIBLE AS AN UNDERGRADUATE, BUT FROM NOTES HE KEPT OF HIS ACCOUNTS AND OTHER SCRAPS OF EVIDENCE IT IS POSSIBLE TO RECONSTRUCT A LITTLE OF HIS LIFE AT THIS TIME.

Leaving Woolsthorpe on June 2 or 3, 1661, Newton journeyed down the Great North Road to Cambridge, enrolling at Trinity on June 5 after a cursory examination by the senior dean and head lecturer. In addition to this he had to enter the university in a process known as matriculation, and on July 8 he joined other students in swearing an oath and paying a fee.

But Newton was not like other students. There was a hierarchy of students based on wealth. At the top were the fellow commoners, wealthy students who could afford privileges such as sitting at the top table in the dining hall; then came pensioners, described by Westfall as "merely affluent." Below these were the untouchables of university life, sizars and subsizars, defined in the statutes of Trinity as "scholars pauperes." Sizars served the master and fellows, while subsizars served fellow students, but they were essentially equivalent: servants, who received a discount on their tuition fees but were not fed by the college. Their job was to perform menial tasks such as acting as valets, polishing boots, waiting table in hall, cleaning, carrying wood, and even emptying chamber pots. A sort of apartheid was imposed by statutes forbidding the subsizars to mingle with the pensioners and commoners.

Short Commons

It was to this lowly station that Newton was condemned, for it his mother chose to restrict his allowance to a pittance. Why she should do this is not clear; her annual income at this time is believed to have been in excess of £700, which would have made her one of the richest women in the county, if not the country, yet it appears from his accounts that she allowed Isaac just £10 a year. Perhaps she resented being bullied into sending him to university, or was somehow trying to punish him for abandoning his domestic duties.

The effect was to inflict upon Newton an outcast existence. At least a year older than the other subsizars, he was also separated from them by his relatively wealthy background and intellectual precocity. Evidence from his expenses suggests that he attempted to act above his "station," spending money on expensive clothes and paying to sit at a higher table. He also lent money to pensioners; in itself this was not unusual, but Newton's own records show that he did not lend to fellow sizars or subsizars.

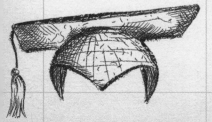

Under the Puritans square caps of the sort shown here were considered Catholic, and disappeared in favor of round ones. After the Restoration the mortarboards had made a comeback.

This engraving, which surfaced in 1799, was claimed to be a portrait of the undergraduate Newton by Sir Peter Lely. In fact it looks nothing like Newton and is probably not even by Lely.

"My father's Intimacy with Him came by mere accident: My Father's first Chamber-Fellow being very disagreeable to him, he retired one day into the Walks, where he found Mr Newton solitary and dejected; Upon entering into discourse they found their cause of Retirement the same, & thereupon agreed to shake off their present disorderly Companions and Chum together, which they did as soon as they conveniently could..."

— ACCOUNT OF THE MEETING OF NEWTON AND JOHN WICKINS BY THE LATTER'S SON, NICHOLAS WICKINS, 1728

Does Not Mix Well with Others

Despite these apparent attempts to ingratiate himself with higher-ranked students, the evidence is that he was miserable and solitary. In 1662 his list of recent sins included "Using Wilfords towel to spare my own" and "Denying my chamber-fellow of the knowledge of him that took him for a sot," suggesting he did not get on with his roommate.

This solitary nature is borne out by the account of how, probably in early 1663, he met John Wickins, with whom he formed the only significant undergraduate relationship of his years at Cambridge. The account suggests he had been unhappy with his roommate for at least 18 months; as Westfall comments, "The sober, silent, thinking lad of Grantham had become the solitary and dejected scholar of Cambridge."

But perhaps his time there was not one of unrelieved misery, for his accounts also reveal that later in his university career he visited at least one tavern and even wagered money at cards; practically the only records of his lifetime showing Newton enjoying normal leisure pursuits.

Old School vs. the New Philosophy

CAMBRIDGE WAS A GREAT UNIVERSITY BUT, IN THE EARLY 1660S, A POOR PLACE FOR LEARNING, CLINGING TO AN ANTIQUATED AND OBSOLETE CURRICULUM THAT HINDERED RATHER THAN ADVANCED NEWTON'S EDUCATION IN NATURAL PHILOSOPHY. YET THE GREAT LIBRARY OF TRINITY, AND THE CLUTCH OF FORWARD-THINKING SCHOLARS AT THE UNIVERSITY, OFFERED YOUNG MEN LIKE ISAAC A WAY INTO A NEW WORLD OF THINKING, A WORLD WHERE GREAT DISCOVERIES AWAITED.

By the time of Newton's arrival Cambridge University was more than 400 years old. Originally founded as an offshoot of Oxford, it had flourished under Elizabeth I and James I, its population multiplying four- or fivefold, until it outstripped its forebear. It became the intellectual powerhouse of English Puritanism, but as a degree became one of the primary means to access state or religious office, so the university became little more than a "degree mill."

Scholasticism

If this was not calculated to enhance its role as a place of learning, still worse was the antiquated curriculum, which largely dated back to the Middle Ages and still adhered to the medieval school of philosophy known as scholasticism. Scholasticism taught that the only path to knowledge and truth was through pure, abstract reason. Learning from experiments and looking at what actually happened in the real world—collectively known as empiricism—were regarded with contempt.

Above all, the curriculum focused on the work of one man, the ancient Greek philosopher Aristotle. "The reading of Aristotle will not only conduce much to your study … but allso help you in Greeke, & indeed crown all your other learning," wrote Richard Holdsworth in his *Directions for a Student in the University*, a contemporary study guide. Aristotle taught that motion was a change in the properties of a substance; it included a stone falling to the ground, a child growing into an adult, water boiling on a fire, even the ripening of fruit, or the moulding of clay into a pot. He asserted that "Everything that is in motion must be moved by something," and

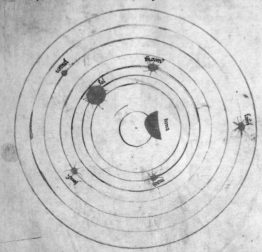

A diagrammatic representation of the Ptolemaic cosmology, in a 15th-century work, showing the concentric crystalline spheres of the heavens centered on the Earth, with the Sun, the Moon, and the planets, all surrounded by the stars. These spheres were said to be immutable.

"Amicus Plato amicus Aristoteles magis amica veritas."
"Plato is my friend, Aristotle is my friend, but truth is my greater friend."

— EPIGRAPH INSCRIBED BY NEWTON IN HIS NOTEBOOK, ADAPTING A PHRASE OF ARISTOTLE'S, WHO HAD SAID, "PLATO IS MY FRIEND, BUT TRUTH MY GREATER FRIEND." NEWTON HERE STATED HIS COMMITMENT TO THE NEW PHILOSOPHICAL SPIRIT OF INQUIRY, WHICH SUPERSEDED THE OLD, ARISTOTLE-FIXATED SCHOOL OF SCHOLASTICISM.

that all motion can therefore be traced back to its original or first mover. Christian theology had adopted this philosophy as a proof of the existence of God. But Aristotelian philosophy did not allow room for any actual science of motion; it ignored or disapproved of attempts to measure qualities and quantities such as speed and acceleration.

The scholastic system also enshrined as dogma the Aristotelian cosmology, as developed by the ancient philosopher Ptolemy. The Earth was at the center of the universe and the heavens were essentially immutable, concentric crystal spheres that encased it.

A Whole New World

Like all the other undergraduates Newton embarked on the study of this medieval curriculum, making notes on Aristotle in a new notebook he purchased. But even before he reached Cambridge he had begun to learn of the new philosophy that was challenging the old dogma. Once there, he was able to read the works of men like Copernicus, Kepler, Bacon, Galileo, and Descartes.

Copernicus had advanced a heliocentric system (a system in which the planets revolve around the Sun) and Kepler had employed mathematics to describe the elliptical motion of the planets. Galileo, through experiments and astronomical observations, had shown that hard evidence challenged scholastic dogma. The great French philosopher René Descartes had advanced the notion of a mechanical universe—one explicable purely through mechanics. And the Elizabethan sage Sir Francis Bacon had urged the adoption of inductive reasoning in the scientific quest for knowledge, in which observations were used to derive principles or laws. From these men the torch of the new philosophy would pass to Newton; in his hands it would burn brighter than ever before.

Phenomena such as comets contradicted the scholastic, Ptolemaic dogma of a fixed cosmology in which new events and objects, such as comets, were supposed to be impossible.

Certain Philosophical Questions

NEWTON'S FIRST STEPS IN SCIENCE TOOK THE FORM OF A SERIES OF QUESTIONS HE WROTE DOWN IN A NOTEBOOK HE HAD BOUGHT IN HIS FIRST YEAR TO TAKE NOTES ON ARISTOTELIAN LOGIC AND ETHICS, WHICH FILLED THE FRONT AND BACK OF THE BOOK. IN HIS SECOND YEAR HE STARTED AGAIN IN THE MIDDLE OF THE BOOK, AND WROTE THE HEADING "QUESTIONES QUEDAM PHILOSOPHICAE" ("CERTAIN PHILOSOPHICAL QUESTIONS").

One of Newton's strengths was the systematic way he approached problems. He often began the same way; by researching what was already known about a subject, and by making notes in which he interrogated and challenged this information. In this early notebook (known as the Philosophical Notebook) he used what he had read of both the old and new philosophies to formulate 45 headings that summarized the state of knowledge in natural philosophy. The headings constituted something more, however: a research program for a new natural philosophy, a plan of attack on the most fundamental problems in nature.

Of Atoms and Space

Newton started at the beginning: "Of the First Matter. Of Atoms." What was matter composed of, what was its nature? "Whither it be mathematical points: or Mathematical points & parts: or a simple entity before division indistinct: or individuals i.e. Atoms." This was a debate that had raged in ancient Greece, where Democritus had advanced an atomic theory. Aristotle, 75 years later, had championed a rival theory; that all matter was composed of four essential elements, and it was this theory that had become the orthodoxy up until Newton's time. The same theory also explained gravity; it was a property of air and fire that they should rise above water and earth, so that the reason that an apple fell to the ground was because its watery/earthy nature caused it to seek its natural place in the order of things.

But Newton's reasoning led him to a different conclusion. "It remains therefore that the first matter must be atoms," he wrote, "And that Matter may be so small as to be indiscernible." Here he broached an important idea. Atoms were things that were almost infinitely small, but not quite; infinitesimal, but not zero: a concept that would serve him well when he came to formulate calculus (see pages 48–9).

Under the heading "Of Time & Eternity" he drew simply "The representation of a clock to go by water or sand." Under the heading "Of Motion" he tried to work out what the basic element of motion could be. From here he moved on to consider "Celestial Matter & Orbs."

"Nothing can be divided into more parts than it can possibly be constituted of. But [finite] matter cannot be constituted of infinite parts."

—NEWTON, FROM THE PHILOSOPHICAL NOTEBOOK

Descartes' Mechanistic Philosophy

This brought him to a discussion of the theories of the French philosopher Descartes, and his massively influential mechanistic philosophy. In the universe according to Descartes, there was no such thing as a vacuum; all space was filled with matter, even if most of it was an invisibly subtle form of matter called ether. Grosser bodies, such as planets, moved through this ether, causing swirling vortices as they went, like a boat moving through the water. These vortices in turn transferred energy and force to other bodies, and this explained how objects that appeared not to be in direct contact could in fact directly affect one another. Thus all matter and force in the universe interacted mechanically, and there was no need to invoke mystical or occult concepts like action at a distance, where objects influenced each other through forces that jumped across the intervening space.

In his notebook Newton considered Descartes' "impact physics" model. Could it truly explain the motion of the planets and comets? Elsewhere he pondered varying definitions of a word that was becoming increasingly current in philosophical discussions, "gravity," and discussed what kind of force could make a cannonball travel through the air. He was groping his way toward a unified understanding of all these problems.

René Descartes (1596–1650), the "father of modern philosophy," whose skeptical challenge to the scholastic orthodoxy paved the way for a new generation of philosophers.

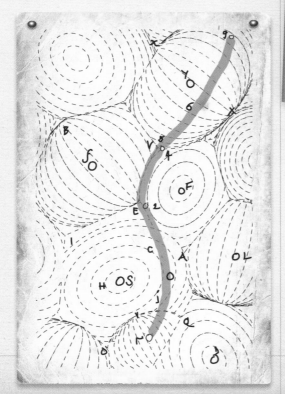

A Cartesian view of space, filled with vortices in the ether so that there is no true vacuum and forces are transmitted through contact—sometimes known as an "impact physics" model.

A Question of Light

"SIR I. BOUGHT A PRISM AT STOURBRIDGE FAIR TO TRY SOME EXPERIMENTS UPON DESCARTES' BOOKS OF COLOURS," READS JOHN CONDUITT'S ACCOUNT OF THE BEGINNING OF MODERN EXPERIMENTAL SCIENCE. NEWTON'S PURCHASE OF WHAT WAS ESSENTIALLY A TOY—A SMALL TRIANGULAR SHAFT OF GLASS—SIGNALED HIS INTENT NOT ONLY TO CHALLENGE AUTHORITY, FOR HE WAS NOT CONTENT TO TAKE DESCARTES AT HIS WORD, BUT ALSO TO IMPLEMENT A RADICAL NEW ROUTE TO TRUTH.

Stourbridge Fair, held a little way outside of Cambridge at the end of the navigable waterways from the Fens to the east, was the greatest fair in all England, described by one pamphleteer as "an Abstract of all sorts of mankind." Newton visited it in 1664 and bought his prism and some books. He was now deep into the new learning, but even as Descartes' philosophy had challenged centuries of scholastic dogma, so Newton was ready to challenge the Frenchman's authority. Where Descartes had considered the world and thought up hypotheses to explain it, trusting to logic and the force of his intelligence, Newton was unwilling to accept anything as true unless he could prove it for himself.

Above all, he was aware of the vital importance of experimentation. As he explained in his notebook under the heading "Philosophy":

"The nature of things is more securely and naturally deduced from their operations one upon another than upon the senses. And when by the former experiments we have found the nature of bodies ... we may more clearly find the nature of the senses."

In other words, the philosopher could not simply sit at his desk and base his theories on what he thought he knew. The best, "more secure" way to discover the nature of things was to observe "their operations one upon another," and this meant performing experiments.

Light and Color

Descartes had proposed a theory of light and color. Light, he said, was a form of pressure ("pression" in the language of the time) through the transparent ether. An object was visible because vortices in the ether transmitted "light pressure" from the object to the eye.

Newton began by copying out passages from Descartes, but followed these with a number of objections that quickly demolished the great man's theory:

"Light cannot be by pression for then wee should see in the night as well or better than in the day. We should see a bright light about us because we are pressed downwards ... A man going or running, would see in the night."

Eclipses would be impossible, he pointed out, because in Descartes' theory ether had to be subtle enough to flow unhindered through all bodies, even planets, and since ether transmitted light pressure this would mean that light too could pass through planets.

DESCARTES THE SKEPTIC

One of Descartes' most profound legacies to Newton was his epistemology (system of enquiry). He challenged the syllogistic reasoning of the scholastics, in which conclusions are based on premises, which must be true in order for the conclusions to be valid. Descartes pointed out that since premises are dependent on fallible senses, they can only be "believed" and not "known"; hence syllogistic reasoning can lead only to doubt. He turned to geometry as a source of epistemological certainty.

"To know how swift light is. Set a broad well polished looking glass on a high steeple so that with a Telescope 1, 2, 3, 10, or 20 miles off you may see your self in it & having by you a great candle in the night cover it & uncover it & observe how long tis before you see the [light go out]."

Newton describes an idea for an experiment to measure the speed of light. In order for this to work one would need to be a great deal further away from the mirror and have a very great candle.

He mused on other consequences that would follow from Descartes' theory: "Whither the rays of light may not move a body as wind doth a mill sail [?]" And he began to consider the matter of color, in which he would make his first scientific breakthrough. According to Aristotle, colors resulted from mixtures of darkness and light. But if this were so, Newton reasoned, "pictures drawn with [black] ink [on white paper] would be coloured or … would seem coloured at a distance & the verges of shadows would be coloured." In fact, he pointed out, "No colour will arise out of the mixture of pure black & white." Existing theories were clearly inadequate. What was needed was a new theory, but one based on experiment and observation, not flawed assumptions.

Beams of subtle light particles stream through the ether.

The connection between the material brain and the immaterial mind is the pineal gland.

Mind sends messages to move arm via pineal gland.

Descartes thought that vision was the result of light particles reflecting off objects and impressing themselves onto the eye, from whence the pressure was transmitted to the pineal gland.

Some Experiments in Optics

NEWTON USED THE PRISM BOUGHT FROM STOURBRIDGE FAIR TO TRY SOME SIMPLE EXPERIMENTS IN HIS ROOM. HE KNEW FROM DESCARTES AND OTHER SOURCES THAT LIGHT WAS REFRACTED (BENT OR DEFLECTED) WHEN IT PASSED FROM ONE MEDIUM TO ANOTHER (FOR EXAMPLE, FROM AIR TO GLASS) AND ALSO THAT ON PASSING THROUGH A PRISM IT WAS REFRACTED TO GIVE A RAINBOW OF COLORS; "A VERY PLEASING DIVERTISSE-MENT" NEWTON CALLED IT, BUT HE QUICKLY USED THE "DIVERTISSEMENT" TO FORMULATE A NEW THEORY OF REFLECTED COLOR.

The spectrum of colors produced by the prism demonstrated to Newton that white light was being split into different components. As he looked at the spectrum he could see that blue light, at one end of the spectrum, was evidently bent or refracted more than red light, at the other. He was also able to judge (although not necessarily at this point to prove) that the color of an object depended on which parts of the spectrum it absorbed and which it reflected. He wrote in his Philosophical Notebook:

"Hence redness yellowness &c are made in bodies by stopping the slowly moved rays without much hindering of the motion of the swifter rays. & blue green & purple by diminishing the motion of the swifter rays & not of the slower."

When he spoke of slower and swifter, he meant more or less refracted, so that blue was "slower" and red was "swifter." Thus if an object ("body") absorbed ("stopped") slow blue rays but reflected ("did not hinder") swift red ones, it would appear red, and vice versa. Different substances reflect or absorb different parts of the spectrum, and this is what gives them their color. Today this is accepted as the true explanation for what is known as "physical color."

Blinded by Science

Newton plunged deeper into optical researches, displaying a reckless enthusiasm for experiment that demonstrates how easily his single-mindedness could turn into obsession and verge on madness. At first his experiments sound charming, "A feather or a black riband put between my eye and the setting Sun makes glorious colours" (the closely spaced tines of the feather act as a diffraction grating), but then they become dangerous.

Curious as to whether "my Phantasie & the Sun had the same operation upon the spirits in my optick nerve & that the same motions are caused in my braines by both," he did what every schoolchild knows one shouldn't. He later described the incident to his friend the philosopher John Locke:

The tines of a feather act as a diffraction grating—light waves refracting around the tines interfere with each other to amplify or suppress wavelengths and produce bands of light and dark.

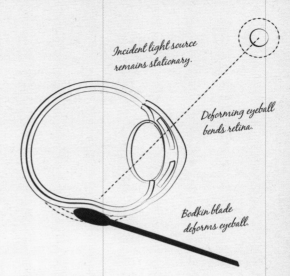

Incident light source remains stationary.

Deforming eyeball bends retina.

Bodkin blade deforms eyeball.

AN EXPERIMENT TOO FAR?

A year later he tried an even more dangerous experiment. Desiring to test whether compression of the eyeball would change the perception of color, he stuck a bodkin (a small, thin-bladed dagger) "betwixt my eye and the bone as near to the backside of my eye as I could: & pressing my eye with the end of it ... there appeared several white, dark, and coloured circles. Which circles were plainest when I continued to rub my eye with the point of the bodkin..."

"I procured me a triangular-glass prism, to try therewith the celebrated Phenomena of Colours. And in order thereto having darkened my chamber, and made a small hole in my window-shuts, to let in a convenient quantity of the sun's light, I placed my prism at its entrance, that it might be thereby refracted to the opposite wall. It was at first a very pleasing divertissement, to view the vivid and intense colours produced thereby..."

— NEWTON TO HENRY OLDENBURG, SECRETARY OF THE ROYAL SOCIETY, 1672

"I looked a very little while upon the Sun in a looking glass with my right eye & then turned my eyes into a dark corner of my chamber and then winked to observe the impression made... This I repeated a second & a third time... And now in a few hours time I had brought my eyes to such a pass that I could look upon no bright object with either eye but I saw [the Sun] before me, so that I dared neither write nor read but to recover the use of my eyes shut myself up in my chamber made dark for three days together & used all means to divert my imagination from the Sun."

A Mathematical Education

ALTHOUGH THE CURRICULUM AT CAMBRIDGE DID NOT FEATURE MUCH MATHEMATICS, IT WAS POSSIBLE FOR STUDENTS TO TAP INTO THE EXCITING DEVELOPMENTS THAT WERE OCCURRING ACROSS EUROPE. JUST A YEAR AFTER NEWTON'S ARRIVAL THE LUCASIAN CHAIR OF MATHEMATICS HAD BEEN ESTABLISHED; IN 1664 ITS FIRST INCUMBENT, PROFESSOR ISAAC BARROW, BEGAN GIVING LECTURES. NEWTON MEANWHILE WAS PURSUING HIS OWN CRASH COURSE IN MATHEMATICS: IN LESS THAN 18 MONTHS HE MASTERED THE ENTIRE BODY OF MATHEMATICS KNOWN TO THE WEST.

Like many geniuses in history, Newton was largely self-taught. The account of how he learned his mathematics—recorded by French mathematician Abraham De Moivre in 1727—is a classic of its kind:

"In '63 [Newton] being at Stourbridge fair bought a book of astrology to see what was there in it. Read it 'til he came to a figure of the heavens which he could not understand for want of being acquainted with trigonometry. Bought a book of trigonometry, but was not able to understand the demonstrations. Got Euclid to fit himself for understanding the ground of trigonometry. Read only the titles of the propositions, which he found so easy to understand that he wondered how anybody would amuse themselves to write any demonstrations of them."

John Conduitt takes up the story: "He bought Descartes's Geometry & read it by himself. When he was got over 2 or 3 pages he could understand no farther then he began again & got 3 or 4 pages farther till he came to another difficult place, then he began again & advanced farther & continued so doing till he made himself Master of the whole without having the least light or instruction from any body."

An Indifferent Opinion

De Moivre further commented that "[Newton] despised [Euclid's works] as a trifling book..." which seems an abrupt dismissal of the man known as the "father of geometry."

His contempt, however, would backfire in April 1664 when it came to gaining the exam passes he would need in order to qualify as an undergraduate scholar, fit to sit for a bachelor of arts degree the following year. His tutor Benjamin Pulleyn, remarkable in this story only for the absence of any impact he made upon his young charge, decided that, since Newton was more interested in mathematics than the official curriculum, the right man to examine him was the Lucasian professor of mathematics, Isaac Barrow. Barrow duly quizzed Newton on what he probably assumed to be the most basic material possible, with results that nearly proved disastrous for the young man's university career. Conduitt relates the story:

"... the Dr examined him in Euclid which Sir I. had neglected & knew little or nothing of, & never asked him about Descartes' Geometry which he was master of." — JOHN CONDUITT

"When he stood to be a scholar of the house his tutor sent him to Dr Barrow then Mathematical professor to be examined, the Dr examined him in Euclid which Sir I. had neglected & knew little or nothing of, & never asked him about Descartes' Geometry which he was master of. Sir I. was too modest to mention it himself & Dr Barrow could not imagine that one could have read that book without being first master of Euclid, so that Dr Barrow conceived then but an indifferent opinion of him but however he was made scholar of the house."

Isaac Barrow, the first Lucasian professor of mathematics.

Friends in High Places

How did Newton overcome this "indifferent opinion"? Conduitt does not explain, but most Newton scholars perceive the hand of Humphrey Babington. Babington was a senior fellow at the college and had a great deal of pull because he was known to enjoy the favor of King Charles. As Westfall points out: "Four years earlier, the Reverend William Ayscough and Mr Stokes had rescued Newton from rural oblivion. Someone performed that service again in April 1664, and on the whole Humphrey Babington appears most likely to have been the one."

In 1699 Newton set down a brief account of what happened next, demonstrating how quickly he now progressed:

"By consulting an account of my expenses at Cambridge in the years 1663 and 1664 I find that in the year 1664 I bought Schooten's Miscellanies & Cartes Geometry (having read this Geometry & Oughtred's Clavis above half a year before) & borrowed Wallis's works & by consequence made these Annotations out of Schooten & Wallis in winter between those years 1664 & 1665."

"A Vulgar Mechanick can practice what he has been taught or seen done, but if he is in an error he knows not how to find it out and correct it, and if you put him out of his road, he is at a stand; Whereas he that is able to reason nimbly and judiciously about figure, force and motion, is never at rest till he gets over every rub."

A fragment of Euclid's *Elements*, the work of an author and mathematician whom Newton considered to be "trifling."

CHAPTER THREE

PLAGUE
AND
PROFESSORSHIP

The Plague Years

IN THE WINTER OF **1664** A COMET APPEARED IN THE NIGHT SKY. TO NEWTON AND A HANDFUL OF OTHER NATURAL PHILOSOPHERS IT WAS AN OBJECT OF INTENSE SCIENTIFIC INTEREST; HOWEVER, FOR MUCH OF THE REST OF THE POPULATION IT WAS A GRIM PORTENT OF DOOM—A HERALD OF PLAGUE. NEWTON FOUND REFUGE AT WOOLSTHORPE, TOGETHER WITH THE THINKING SPACE THAT WOULD USHER IN A YEAR OF MIRACLES: HIS *ANNUS MIRABILIS.*

Sometime in 1665 a ship from continental Europe or the Mediterranean docked in London, carrying in its hold rats, which in turn carried fleas, which in turn carried virulent bubonic plague bacteria. People began to die with frightening speed; rumors and fear spread throughout the capital and the country. Newton's mother wrote from Woolsthorpe, concerned. Her letter, damaged, sketchily literate and with words missing, is a rare testament from his early life to something approaching a normal, loving relationship:

Isack

received your leter and I perceive you letter from me with your cloth but none to you your sisters present thai love to you with my motherly lov you and prayers to god for you I your loving mother
— hannah, wollstrup, May 6, 1665

Just a few days earlier Samuel Pepys had noted in his diary: "Great fears of sickness here in the City, it being said that two or three houses are already shut up." Within weeks the disease was rampant, eventually killing 70,000 Londoners. The rest of the country got off relatively lightly, the plague claiming only 30,000 lives as towns and cities implemented strict quarantines.

Cambridge shut up shop; Stourbridge Fair was canceled in both 1665 and 1666. The stringent measures proved effective: the "Plague Bill" for June 5 to January 1 was relatively light, with only 749 dead, and around 370 who contracted it but survived. The colleges in particular seem to have escaped mostly unscathed, probably as so many of the students and fellows went home, among them the 22-year-old Newton.

The diarist Samuel Pepys, who remained in London during the plague. He later served as president of the Royal Society.

"All this was in the two plague years 1665 and 1666, for in those days I was in the prime of my age for invention, and minded mathematics and philosophy more than at any time since."

Annus Mirabilis

In late June or early July Newton returned home to Woolsthorpe. Presumably Hannah had by now accepted that her son was not fitted for farm labor, for he was afforded the leisure to devote himself utterly and without distraction to his mathematical and philosophical musings. Later in life, when asked how he achieved his mental breakthroughs, Newton explained: "I keep the subject constantly before me and wait 'till the first dawnings open slowly, by little and little, into a full and clear light." This kind of single-minded application to a problem is a hallmark of genius and has been the key to many scientific breakthroughs. As Newton himself later remarked, "Truth is the offspring of silence and meditation." The result of this leisure was a period of intellectual productivity that has gone down in legend as his *annus mirabilis*, although in practice this "year" lasted somewhere between 18 and 24 months.

Opening the Waste Book

Newton still possessed the large book of mostly blank sheets of paper that he had inherited from his stepfather, Barnabas Smith, which he called his Waste Book. It was in this that he began to make notes on geometry, algebra, and the great problems then current in mathematics—the mathematics of curves, in particular how to work out the gradient of a curve and the area under a curve. Curves describe the properties and actions of moving bodies, so to be able to manipulate and calculate them meant, by extension, being able to understand and describe concepts such as force and acceleration, and, above all, the motion of the planets.

NEWTON'S ACHIEVEMENT
Historians of science are still in awe of how much was achieved in so little time. According to D.T. Whiteside, the pre-eminent expert on Newton's mathematics, "Never did seventeenth-century man build up so great a store of mathematical expertise, much of his own discovery, in so short a time," while another Newton scholar, Derek Gjertsen, wrote that: "in a remarkably short period the twenty-four-year-old student created modern mathematics, mechanics, and optics. There is nothing remotely like it in the history of thought."

Inventing Calculus

CALCULUS IS A MATHEMATICAL TOOL FOR WORKING WITH CURVES, IN PARTICULAR FOR CALCULATING THE GRADIENT OF A CURVE AND THE AREA UNDER IT, FEATS THAT HAD BEEN BEYOND THE ANCIENT GREEKS AND WHICH WERE EXERCISING THE GREATEST MINDS IN EUROPE WHEN NEWTON TURNED HIS ATTENTION TO THE PROBLEM IN 1665–6. HIS DISCOVERIES IN THIS FIELD ALONE WOULD HAVE ENSURED THE IMMORTALITY OF HIS NAME.

Curved lines, such as those described by a ball thrown through the air, or a planet going around the Sun, were of great interest to mathematicians. Working with the system of algebra developed by medieval Islamic scholars, Descartes had shown how to describe geometrical forms using algebraic terms (such as x and y) to represent what came to be known as "Cartesian coordinates," and how they could be drawn using axes and graphs.

A graph of a straight line has properties that are easy to work out. Formulae known since ancient Babylonian times can calculate the area under a straight line, while its gradient—the rate of change described by the slope of the line—is simply the change in values of its y coordinates divided by the corresponding change in x coordinates. But for a curve these properties are much harder to work out. Mathematicians before Newton realized that one way to do it was to calculate approximations, by imagining a curve as a series of shifting straight lines (tangents), and the area under the curve as a series of rectangles and triangles. Using ever more and smaller rectangles and triangles (known as "squaring the curve" or "quadrature") would allow a closer approximation, but it would still be only an approximation.

Squaring the Curve

Newton had begun his assault on this problem even before his return to Woolsthorpe, while he was still a junior at college in February 1665. He knew that the French mathematician Pierre de Fermat and his own professor, Barrow, had both described solutions for specific curves, and he began to wonder how it could be generalized to all curves. "I had the hint of this method from Fermat's way of drawing tangents and by applying it to abstract equations, directly and invertedly, I made it general," he later wrote.

The key to the problem was his ability to work with infinite series. Newton realized that, rather than adding up to infinity, a sum involving infinite series would close in on a finite goal or limit, and that this could be used to square a curve—effectively, using an infinite number of infinitely small rectangles to give the area under a curve. From this he was able to develop "a Method whereby to square those crooked lines which may be squared"; today this method is called integration.

The most prominent example of a problem in circular motion was the orbit of the planets (although Kepler had shown that their orbits were actually elliptical).

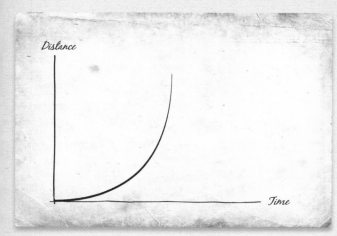

Distance

Time

A graph of the accelerating velocity of an object dropped from a tower. The gradient of the curve equals the velocity of the object.

INFINITE SERIES

Infinite series are sums made up of an infinite number of terms. For instance, suppose you and a friend are asked to shut a door, but to take it in turns to close it by half the distance it is open, then half of that distance, and so on. First you would close it half the total distance, then your friend would close it a quarter of the total distance, then you by an eighth of the total distance, and so on. The door would only be closed when all these fractions add up to one. Each fraction is a "term" in the sum, and each term represents you and your friend taking a turn to shut the door halfway. How many turns would it take for you and your friend to shut the door?

Resolving Problems by Motion

Integration is one part of calculus; its mirror image is the operation now known as differentiation, which is a way of calculating the gradient of a curve. The fundamental theorem of calculus is that the two operations are inversions of one another. Newton was the first to understand this, and he arrived at this understanding because he was able to see how geometrical problems—gradients of curves—were also problems of kinetics, of moving things.

If you draw a graph of a ball falling from a tower, with the y-axis representing its position and the x-axis representing the time since you dropped it, you will get a curved line. The gradient of the curve will show how the speed of the ball is increasing over time. In other words it will be a measure of acceleration, the rate at which the speed is changing. But speed itself is also a measure of rate of change; in other words, the gradient of the curve is a measure of the rate of change of the rate of change. In discovering how to work out this acceleration, Newton mastered differentiation. Under the heading "To resolve problems by motion" he set out a series of propositions proving his new theory, inventing new words to describe the concepts: "fluents" and "fluxions." He called his new system the theory of fluxions.

"I am ashamed to tell to how many places I carried these computations, having no other business at that time; for then I took really too much delight in these inventions."

Discovering Gravity

NEWTON IS MOST FAMOUS FOR DISCOVERING GRAVITY, THE FUNDAMENTAL FORCE OF NATURE THAT KEEPS THE PLANETS IN THEIR ORBITS AND CAUSES APPLES TO FALL TO THE GROUND. BEFORE NEWTON THE DISCUSSION OF SUCH FORCES HAD BEEN A MATTER OF SPECULATION AND FANTASY, OF TENDENCIES AND QUALITIES; AFTER HIM FORCE COULD BE QUANTIFIED AND CALCULATED. THE SUMS HE CREATED WOULD BE USED TO FIRE ROCKETS INTO SPACE AND PUT MEN ON THE MOON.

What do we mean when we say that Newton "discovered" gravity? The phenomenon of gravity was apparent enough, and the word itself was coming into use at that time to describe whatever property it was that made some things tend earthwards. Newton's breakthrough was to discover a precise, mathematical quantification of the force of gravity, and to prove that it operated as a fundamental force of attraction between all things. In his day he was most celebrated for elucidating the inverse square law of gravity, and this is what is generally meant when it is said that Newton discovered gravity.

The Inverse Square Law

The inverse square law of gravity says that the gravitational attraction between two objects varies according to one divided by the square of the distance between them ("inverse" in this context means dividing into one; another term used is "reciprocal"; in mathematical notation this would be written as $\frac{1}{x^2}$ or x^{-2}). For instance, imagine that three planets of equal mass orbit the Sun: Planet A at a distance of one Astronomical Unit (AU); Planet B at a distance of two AU; and Planet C at a distance of three AU. Planet B is twice as far away, so the force of attraction

A depiction of the Copernican, heliocentric model of cosmology, showing the Earth and the other planets orbiting the Sun. Jupiter is shown with its Galilean moons.

will be $\frac{1}{2^2} = \frac{1}{4}$ of that experienced by Planet A. Planet C is three times as far away, so the force will be $\frac{1}{3^2} = \frac{1}{9}$ of that experienced by Planet A. A planet that was four times as far away from the Sun as Planet A would experience $\frac{1}{16}$ the attraction, and so on.

So how did Newton arrive at this rule? According to the legend of the apple he was struck with it all at once—a flash of insight, perhaps even of divine inspiration. In truth, the process was much more drawn-out and halting. Thanks to his mathematical breakthroughs he now had the tools to work with curves and circles, and most of all to solve the mysteries of circular motion.

A Thought Experiment

Using these tools he considered a thought experiment: if a stone tied on the end of a string is whirled around in a circle it experiences two opposing forces. One force, known as the "centrifugal" or "receding" force, tries to make the stone fly off, while another (the "centripetal" or "attractive" force, exerted by the string) pulls it toward the center of the circle. The two forces cancel each other out so that the stone travels in a circular orbit, but if the string is cut then the stone will fly off in a straight line.

The ball travels in a circle instead of flying off, because the attractive and receding forces are equal.

Newton desired to calculate the exact receding force acting on the stone; by doing so he would also be working out the attractive force. For his calculations he imagined the stone as a sphere rolling around the inside of a bigger sphere. Using his new mathematical tools he was able to calculate the exact receding force exerted every time it made a revolution, and he was able to link this to the size of the circle the stone described; in other words, its orbit. There was an inverse square relationship between the two.

From a stone whirling in a circle, it was but a short conceptual leap to the planets orbiting the Sun. But what would prompt such a leap? Would the relationship between the orbits the planets described and the receding force they experienced also obey an inverse square rule? Like the stone on the string, the planets must be experiencing an attractive force equal to the receding force. Therefore the answer to the first question would also be the answer to the question: "would the relationship between the orbits of the planets and the attractive force keeping them in those orbits obey an inverse square law?" But how could Newton find out whether his model fitted the facts?

GRAVITY BEFORE NEWTON

Aristotelian physics explained that gravity was the result of a predominance of earthly and watery humors in an object's makeup, and that objects therefore had a tendency to seek their "rightful place" in the scheme of things. In reality, however, this was no explanation at all, and was based on unfounded and untested—perhaps untestable—assumptions about the nature of matter.

"[I] found out how to estimate the force with which a globe revolving within a sphere presses the surface of the sphere..."

— FROM NEWTON'S MEMORANDUM, c.1714

Fruit of Legend: Newton's Apple

POPULAR LEGEND HAS IT THAT NEWTON WAS LITERALLY STRUCK BY THE CONCEPT OF GRAVITY WHEN AN APPLE FELL ON HIS HEAD. VISITORS TO WOOLSTHORPE CAN STILL SEE AN APPLE TREE SAID TO HAVE DESCENDED FROM THE TREE OF LORE. IN FACT, NEWTON DID TELL A NUMBER OF PEOPLE THAT HIS BREAKTHROUGH WAS RELATED TO THE SIGHT OF AN APPLE, AND IN DOING SO CREATED AN ENDURING MYTH THAT SERVED TO CONCEAL THE ALCHEMICAL TRUTH.

The story of Newton's apple is entirely based on hearsay, although he seems to have told the story to as many as four different people. All versions agree that Newton had his conceptual breakthrough in the garden at Woolsthorpe, and some of them even mention a falling apple.

William Stukeley recalled how he had visited an aged and ailing Newton in London, and the two had walked out into the garden, "under the shade of some apple trees, only he and myself... Amidst other discourse, he told me, he was just in the same situation, as when formerly, the notion of gravitation came into his mind. It was occasioned by the fall of an apple, as he sat in contemplative mood."

The French philosopher Voltaire—who was a great admirer of Newton, though he never met him—told the story at least twice, having learned of it from Newton's niece. In his *Éléments de la Philosophie de Newton* Voltaire says:

"One day in the year 1666, Newton, having returned to the country and seeing the fruits of a tree fall, fell, according to what his niece, Mrs. Conduitt, has told me, into a deep meditation about the cause that thus attracts bodies in the line which, if produced, would pass nearly through the center of the Earth."

John Conduitt's version also mentions an apple falling to the ground, and seems to equate most closely to Newton's own account:

"Whilst he was musing in a garden it came into his thought that the power of gravity (which brought an apple to the ground) was not limited to a certain distance from the earth but that this power must extend much farther than was usually thought. Why not as high as the moon said he to himself..."

Near and Far

The key point is that Newton was able to make the conceptual leap from the terrestrial to the celestial, to see that one and the same force must act on both the mighty sphere of the Moon and the decidedly lesser spheres he saw in his garden. Why did an apple fall toward the center of the Earth and not fly off in a straight line into space, as the stone on the string would when released? Why did the Moon stay in orbit around the Earth, and the planets around the Sun, without flying off into space? The same force that governed the fall of the apple must govern the Moon as it constantly fell away from its tangent, toward the Earth.

From reading Galileo and from carrying out his own experiments Newton knew roughly the force of gravity at the surface

François-Marie Arouet (1694–1778), better known by the pen-name Voltaire.

of the Earth, the force of attraction pulling an apple to the ground. Now he wondered if he could compute "the force requisite to keep the Moon in her Orb with the force of gravity at the surface of the Earth" and whether the two would match up according to his inverse square law. To perform the calculation he needed to know the distance from the Earth to the Moon, a calculation that itself depended on working out the radius of the Earth. Unfortunately, in this respect, Newton depended on poor data, as he used a figure obtained by Galileo that was 400 miles (640 kilometers) too small. As a consequence his results did not match up; it seemed that his concept of gravity could not account for the motion of the Moon on its own and he assumed that other forces, perhaps Descartes' vortices, must also be at work. It was not until he returned to the problem nearly 20 years later when it came to writing the *Principia* that Newton was able to use a more accurate estimate of the radius of the Earth and make his calculation work.

This was not the story he bequeathed to posterity, however, claiming that in his initial calculation of the forces acting on Moon and apple he "found them answer pretty well." Did he have an ulterior motive for perpetuating the legend of the apple? Perhaps it served to distract attention from the true, alchemical inspirations for his theory of gravity.

The frontispiece of Voltaire's *Éléments de la Philosophie de Newton*, showing a somewhat idealized image of the great man at work.

"In the same year (1666) I began to think of gravity extending to the orb of the moon and having found out how to estimate the force with which a globe revolving within a sphere presses the surface of the sphere... I deduced that the forces which keep the planets in their orbs must be reciprocally as the squares of their distances from the centres about which they revolve."

— FROM NEWTON'S MEMORANDUM, c.1714

Let the Good Times Roll

NEWTON RETURNED TO CAMBRIDGE HAVING LAID THE FOUNDATIONS FOR PERHAPS THE GREATEST REVOLUTION IN THE HISTORY OF IDEAS, BUT CAMBRIDGE CARED LITTLE. NEWTON'S FUTURE WAS AT STAKE IN THE UPCOMING FELLOWSHIP ELECTIONS, YET HE SEEMED UNCONCERNED, PERHAPS BECAUSE HE HAD AN ACE UP HIS SLEEVE. THE FELLOWSHIP SECURED, HE EVEN FOUND TIME TO RELAX AND ENJOY THE LEISURELY PURSUITS OF ORDINARY MORTALS: GAMBLING, DRINKING, AND SHOPPING.

In early 1667 fear of the plague abated and the university returned to life. Newton came back to Cambridge a gentleman, having officially acquired the status by attending the Herald's visitation at Grantham. He was now able to sign his name: "Isaack Newton of Wolstropp. Gentleman, aged 23." He had spent nearly two years exploring uncharted seas of natural philosophy, but now he faced the more mundane and pressing concerns common to all undergraduates: exams.

It was crucial to Newton's future that he secure one of the few fellowships available at Trinity; success would allow him to pursue a career in academia, failure would condemn him to a rural life, probably as an obscure parson in a Lincolnshire village.

Crimson Tide

Thanks to the good offices of his mentor Humphrey Babington, however, Newton seems to have regarded the selection process as a mere formality. He bought tools to equip his Cambridge lodgings, made plans for the refurbishment of the chambers he shared with Wickins, and bought an official gown. His complacency was well founded, and in March 1667 he was duly elected a fellow, followed by his master's degree the following spring.

Newton was rapidly climbing the college hierarchy and securing his future at the same time, and for perhaps the only time in his life he seems to have relaxed and let his hair down. His expenses record visits to taverns, the loss of money at cards, new clothes, and the expensive redecoration of his rooms, entirely in crimson. The color obsessed him throughout his life, and even as an old man his home was furnished in crimson drapes, covers, and bedclothes.

Newton's expenses during 1667:

To the Taylor Octob 29. 1667.	2 . 13 . 0
To the Taylor. Iune 10. 1667	1 . 3 . 10
For keeping Christmas	0 . 5 . 0
Lost at cards (twice)	0 . 15 . 0
At the Taverne twice	0 . 3 . 6 .

Teacher's Pet

Despite the profound advances he had made, Newton was losing interest in mathematics at this time and becoming increasingly drawn to the mysteries of alchemy. In August 1669 he made his first trip to London, to stock up on alchemical books and materials. He did not visit the Royal Society, although its members might have been very interested to meet him; by this time word of Newton's discoveries had begun to spread.

The name of Isaac Newton was very slowly becoming known to the wider world, largely thanks to Isaac Barrow, the Lucasian professor of mathematics. Since his return to Cambridge, Newton had begun to forge a close relationship with Barrow, one of the few men at Cambridge who could appreciate his recent achievements, and a very useful ally for an ambitious young scholar.

Barrow must soon have discerned that his young protégé had made some remarkable discoveries and clamored to know more, but ran up against one of Newton's defining characteristics: his obsessive secrecy and possessiveness when it came to his research. He affected to have no interest in the renown his discoveries would win: "For I see not what there is desirable in public esteem, were I able to acquire and maintain it. It would perhaps increase my acquaintance, the thing which I chiefly study to decline." This modesty would soon be put to the test.

An engraving of Isaac Barrow, Newton's academic mentor, who was spreading the word about the young man's discoveries.

"For I see not what there is desirable in public esteem, were I able to acquire and maintain it. It would perhaps increase my acquaintance, the thing which I chiefly study to decline."

PATHOLOGICALLY SHY?

Why was Newton so reluctant to reveal himself? It was partly because of his fear of theft and partly because of his desire to produce fully worked-out systems or models rather than what he would dismiss as mere "hypotheses" (see pages 64–5), but perhaps above all it was because of his horror of dispute, of the possibility of being gainsaid—and possibly even defeated.

News of Remarkable Things

LITTLE BY LITTLE, NEWS OF NEWTON'S IDEAS BEGAN TO LEAK OUT, THANKS TO HIS RELATIONSHIP WITH ISAAC BARROW, THE LUCASIAN PROFESSOR OF MATHEMATICS. BARROW WAS HUNGRY FOR THE SECRETS NEWTON HAD UNCOVERED, PERSUADING HIM TO RELEASE SNIPPETS OF INFORMATION. IN RETURN, NEWTON SENSED THE PROSPECT OF ADVANCEMENT, FOR BARROW WAS A VERY AMBITIOUS MAN, ONE WHOSE FAVOR COULD BE REWARDING.

In September 1668 Barrow received from the mathematician and publisher John Collins a copy of Nicholas Mercator's *Logarithmotechnia*, which described new methods for calculating logarithms from infinite series. Mercator had achieved only one specific example of the general system that Newton had invented, but it was clear even from this that there was a risk others might claim credit for discoveries that Newton had already made.

Barrow showed the book to Newton, who responded with a paper, "On Analysis by Infinite Series." At first he refused to let Barrow send it to Collins, although the professor wrote with news: "A friend of mine here, that hath a very excellent genius to these things brought me the other day some paper, wherein he hath set down methods of calculating the dimensions of magnitudes like that of Mr Mercator concerning the hyperbola, but very general."

A month later Newton relented a little, and Barrow was able to send it, hedged about with cautious words:

"I send you the paper of my friend I promised, which I presume will give you much satisfaction; I pray having perused them so much as you think good, remand them to me; according to his desire, when I asked him the liberty to impart them to you. And I pray give me notice of your receiving them with your soonest convenience ... because I am afraid of them; venturing them by post."

MAN OF LEARNING AND SAGACITY
The Lucasian professor had to give a series of lectures; Barrow had chosen optics as his subject, and Newton was asked to edit them for publication. The younger man complied, despite knowing from his own experiments that Barrow's theories were hopelessly outmoded and incorrect.
He was rewarded with an effusive acknowledgment: "a Man of great Learning and Sagacity, who revised my Copy and noted such things as wanted correction."

Through Barrow's words one can clearly hear Newton fretting; keen to win renown, yet pathologically anxious about exposure to a wider world.

Eventually Newton allowed Barrow to reveal to Collins his identity: "I am glad my friend's paper gave you so much satisfaction. His name is Mr Newton; a fellow of our college, & very young... but of an extraordinary genius & proficiency in these things." Collins, in turn, was allowed to show the paper to select members of the Royal Society, but it was not actually published until 1711.

*"His name is Mr Newton; a fellow of our college, & very young ...
but of an extraordinary genius & proficiency in these things."*

— ISAAC BARROW TO JOHN COLLINS, 1668

A Mathematical Courtship

Now Collins too was hungry for more. He began to court Newton, who responded almost coyly to his requests. Asked for a table resolving equations with three dimensions Newton dismissed the task as "pretty easy and obvious enough. But I cannot persuade my self to undertake the drudgery of making it." On sending Collins a formula for calculating the rate of interest on an annuity, he insisted his name be withheld should it be published.

His modesty notwithstanding, Newton's profile was undergoing a dramatic boost. Barrow was ambitious, but a condition of the Lucasian chair was that he hold no other posts; in order to get on, he needed to move on. So, in 1669, he seized the opportunity to become Royal Chaplain, thereby vacating the Lucasian chair.

Newton was perfectly positioned; Barrow recommended him for the chair and in October, 1669, the young scholar became the Lucasian professor of mathematics. Just five years after nearly failing a basic maths exam he was taking over the professorship of the same man who had so nearly flunked him.

This engraving shows the relatively informal nature of Royal Society gatherings, although it dates from the 18th century, when Newton himself was president.

A meeting of the Royal Society

The Absentminded Professor

NEWTON'S POSITION WAS NOW SECURE; AS PROFESSOR HE WOULD LITERALLY HAVE TO KILL SOMEONE TO GET DISMISSED. HE WAS EXPECTED TO GIVE A FEW LECTURES, AND ALTHOUGH NO ONE CAME TO HEAR THEM PERHAPS THIS SUITED HIM WELL—GIVING HIMSELF ENTIRELY TO HIS RESEARCH, HE LOST HIMSELF IN STUDIES TO THE NEGLECT OF THE WORLD AROUND HIM, BECOMING A FIGURE OF MINGLED RIDICULE AND AWE AROUND THE COLLEGE.

Like his predecessor, Newton was expected to give lectures, and just as his predecessor had, Newton chose to speak on optics, proceeding to dismantle Barrow's theories on the matter: "I judge it will not be unacceptable if I bring the principles of this science to a more strict examination ... [than] what my reverent predecessor has last delivered from this place."

A handful of students turned up for Newton's first lecture; none came to his second. Although he eventually cut his lectures to just one per term, he continued to give them for 17 years, but more often than not he lectured to empty theaters. In 1685 he acquired an assistant, Humphrey Newton, a very distant relation, who later recalled: "So few went to hear him, & fewer that understood him, that oftimes he did in a manner, for want of hearers, read to the walls ... he usually stayed about half an hour; when he had no auditors, he commonly returned in a 4th part of that time or less."

Stockings Untied and Head Scarcely Combed

If he wasn't teaching, what was Newton doing? Numerous anecdotes survive to paint a picture of a stereotypical absentminded professor, so lost in contemplation of philosophy that he scarcely noticed his surroundings. According to Stukeley:

"As when he has been in the hall at dinner, he has quite neglected to help himself, and the cloth has been taken away before he has eaten anything... That when he had friends to entertain at his chamber, if he stept in to his study for a bottle of wine, and a thought came into his head, he would sit down to paper and forget his friends."

Humphrey Newton told similar tales and worse: "He alwayes kept close to his studyes, very rarely went a visiting, & had as few Visiters ... I never knew him take any Recreation or Pastime, either in Riding out to take the Air, Walking, Bowling, or any other Exercise whatever, Thinking all Hours lost, that was not spent in his Studyes, to which he kept so close, that he seldom left his Chamber... He very rarely went to Dine in the Hall unless upon some Publick Dayes, & then if He had not been [re]minded, would go very carelessly, with shoes down at Heels, stockins unty'd, surplice on, & his Head scarcely comb'd..."

A standard depiction of Newton, hard at work with the tools of the geometer's trade.

Sometimes he did not even make it to the hall. "At some seldom Times when he design'd to dine in the Hall, would turn to the left hand, & go out into the street, where making a stop, when he found his Mistake, would hastily turn back, & then sometimes instead of going into the Hall, would return to his Chamber again."

Eureka Moments

Wandering the paths of the college, Newton was known to stop abruptly and trace figures in the dirt with a stick; the other fellows learned to step around these, not wishing to risk destroying some piece of genius. Always his mind was on his studies. "When he has sometimes taken a Turn or two, has made a sudden stand, turn'd himself about, run up the stairs, like another Archimedes, with an [Eureka], fall to write on his Desk standing, without giving himself the Leasure to draw a Chair to sit down in," wrote Humphrey Newton. "I believe he grudg'd that short Time he spent in eating & sleeping."

WE ARE NOT AMUSED
It seems that Professor Isaac was a humorless fellow. "I cannot say I ever saw him laugh, but once," wrote Humphrey Newton, recalling an incident when an acquaintance to whom Newton had lent a copy of Euclid questioned the use of studying it, "Upon which Sir Isaac was very merry." According to Newton's niece, one of his few friendships at this time came to an abrupt end when the fellow "told a loose story about a nun, and then Sir Isaac left off all confidence with him."

"...he ate very sparingly, nay, oftimes he has forget to eat at all, so that going into his Chamber, I have found his Mess untouch'd, of which when I have reminded him, would reply, Have I; & then making to the Table, would eat a bit or two standing, for I cannot say, I ever saw Him sit at Table by himself..."

— HUMPHREY NEWTON, ASSISTANT TO ISAAC NEWTON

Experimentum Crucis

IN HIS FIRST SET OF LECTURES AS LUCASIAN PROFESSOR, NEWTON RETURNED TO HIS OPTICAL EXPERIMENTS OF 1664–5, WHICH HE HAD EXTENDED DURING THE PLAGUE YEARS. HE HAD NOW COMPLETED A SERIES OF EXPERIMENTS WHICH ELEGANTLY AND INCONTRO-VERTIBLY PROVED A NEW THEORY OF LIGHT AND COLOR, IN PARTICULAR AN *EXPERIMEN-TUM CRUCIS*, A LANDMARK OR GUIDE EXPERIMENT. IT WAS PERHAPS THE FIRST PIECE OF TRUE SCIENCE EVER DONE.

Newton considered his prism. Previously it had been thought that white was one color of light, and that some property of the prism itself made the other colors it produced. Aristotle had held that colors were produced by mingling different quantities of black and white; Descartes had thought color was the result of globules of light changing speed; Robert Hooke, perhaps the leading natural philosopher in England up to this point, curator of experiments at the Royal Society, and author of the book *Micrographia*, argued that the two fundamental colors, blue and red, were caused by "an impression on the retina of an oblique and confus'd pulse of light."

Differently Refrangible

In his early experiments with prisms, however, Newton had shown that different colors were bent, or refracted (he used the term "refrangible") to different degrees. Perhaps it appealed to him that here was a property of light that was quantifiable; it could be measured. He continued with his experiments. He set a piece of card over the window of his study with a pinhole to let in a ray of light, which he allowed to shine on the prism; a spectrum of colors was produced on the far wall. By interposing between the prism and the wall another piece of card with a pinhole, he could select just one of the colors from the spectrum, isolating a beam of pure red or blue light and allowing it to project onto a second prism. Although this second prism further refracted each colored beam, it did not produce any more colors. He measured angles and found that blue light was always refracted more than red light, yet refraction itself did not necessarily cause a change of color.

This was the signpost he had been looking for, the *experimentum crucis*. This simple experiment seemed to show that a prism did not create color, it simply separated out individual colors from a combination of all of them (white light), and did so because it refracts light, and different colors of light refract to different degrees, or as Newton put it: "Light consists of Rays differently refrangible."

The Most Wonderful Composition

To prove this new theory of light and color, he conceived two more ingenious experiments. Firstly he set a lens in the path of the spectrum produced by a prism. Where the lens focused the beam it produced a white spot; in other words, by using a lens to recombine the different colored rays he was able to reconstitute the original white light. Finally he set a cogged wheel between the lens and the wall, so that the cogs interrupted the different-colored rays of light emerging from the lens before

A prism splitting white light into a spectrum; the angled glass surfaces refract the light, and the different wavelengths refract to different degrees.

they reached their focus and were recombined; thus he was able to cut out one at a time. Turning the wheel moved the cogs so that one color after another was interrupted; the result was that the spot on the wall changed color accordingly as different components of white light were intercepted.

"The most surprising, and wonderful composition," he concluded, "was that of Whiteness. There is no one sort of Rays which alone can exhibit this. 'Tis ever compounded, and to its composition are requisite all the aforesaid primary Colours, mixed in due proportion." His experiments, he declared, were "the oddest if not the most considerable detection which has hitherto been made in the operations of Nature."

"I have often with Admiration beheld, that all the Colours of the Prism being made to converge, and thereby to be again mixed ... reproduced light, entirely and perfectly white."

A colored engraving shows Newton experimenting with focused rays of light.

A CONVENIENT FICTION

The series of experiments that Newton related in his lectures, and later in a letter to the Royal Society, was presented as a neat narrative of insight, theory, experiment, and confirmation, in which he rapidly proceeded from one step to the next. In fact, he constructed the series over several years, and the process was messy and sometimes inconclusive: it was hard, for instance, to separate precisely the components of the spectrum, or to hold a prism precisely in place when the Sun—the source of the original white beam—was constantly moving in the sky.

The Perfection of Telescopes

NEWTON'S OPTICAL RESEARCH PRODUCED MORE THAN JUST THEORIES. HE WAS ABLE TO PUT HIS INSIGHTS TO PRACTICAL USE, CIRCUMVENTING A FUNDAMENTAL HANDICAP IN THE CONSTRUCTION OF TELESCOPES. THROUGH KEENNESS OF INTELLECT AND MANUAL SKILL HE SUCCEEDED IN BUILDING A DEVICE THAT HAD, UNTIL THEN, BEEN PURELY THEORETICAL: THE FIRST EVER REFLECTING TELESCOPE, A DEVICE THAT WOULD ANNOUNCE HIS ARRIVAL ON THE WORLD STAGE.

In 1608 Hans Lippershey had invented a type of telescope that used lenses to gather and focus light on the user's eye; the lenses achieved this feat through the phenomenon of refraction, and hence the device was known as a refractive telescope. Newton knew from experience that these telescopes were of disappointing quality, producing distorted, fuzzy images. Thanks to his optical researches, he alone knew why: "I saw that the perfection of Telescopes was hitherto limited, not so much for want of glasses truly figured according to the prescriptions of Optick Authors, (which all men have hitherto imagined), as because that Light it self is a Heterogenous mixture of differently refrangible rays."

The problem to which he was alluding is today known as "chromatic aberration." A lens, like a prism, refracts or bends light, but also like a prism it will refract different wavelengths (colors) to different degrees (unless it is ground to a perfection beyond the reach of 17th-century artisans). This means that rays of different wavelengths are not focused on the same point, distorting the image formed.

The Reflecting Telescope

To get around this problem Newton turned to another form of telescope, designs for which had been circulating for a while, but which had never been successfully constructed: a reflecting telescope, which used a parabolic mirror rather than a lens to gather light, thus avoiding the problem of chromatic aberration altogether. Crafting a mirror of sufficient quality, however, was a problem all of its own; the best craftsmen in Britain had already tried and failed. Newton was able to employ his alchemical expertise to concoct an alloy with the perfect combination of reflectivity and hardness (so that it could be polished properly).

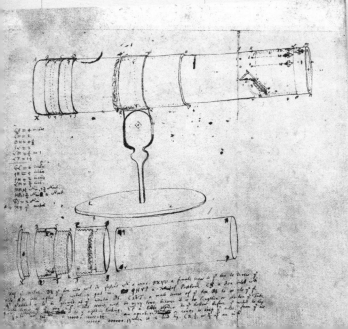

Newton's own sketch of his design for a reflecting telescope, including a breakdown of its components.

"I asked him where he had it made, he said he made it himself, & when I asked him where he got his tools said he made them himself & laughing added if I had staid for other people to make my tools & things for me, I had never made anything..."

— NEWTON ON HAVING MADE THE FIRST REFLECTING TELESCOPE, FROM THE YEAR BEFORE HE DIED; RECOUNTED BY JOHN CONDUITT IN 1726

In February 1669, after exhaustive labors casting, grinding, and polishing the mirror, and crafting the tube, the mount, and other fittings, he succeeded in constructing a stubby device just 6 inches (15 centimeters) long. He wrote to a friend that it could magnify objects "about 40 times in diameter which is more than any 6 foot [1.8 meter] tube [refracting telescope] can do, I believe with distinctness ... I have seen with it Jupiter distinctly round and his satellites, and Venus horned."

Examined and Applauded

Two and a half years later Newton lent his telescope to Barrow, who presented it to the Royal Society in December 1671. The fellows were delighted with it, and the little telescope was carried off to Whitehall to be presented to the king. Henry Oldenburg, Secretary of the Royal Society, wrote to Newton that it had been "examined here by some of the most eminent in optical science and practice, and applauded by them." He assured the Lucasian professor that the Society wished to "secure this invention from the usurpation of foreigners." Newton replied with unconvincing modesty: "At the reading of your letter I was surprised to see so much care taken about securing an invention to me of which I have hitherto had so little value."

On January 11, 1672, Newton was rewarded for his ingenuity by being voted in as a fellow of the Royal Society. Encouraged, he ventured to reveal to the other fellows the theory that had initially prompted the construction of the telescope:

"...I am purposing them, to be considered of & examined, an account of a philosophical discovery which induced me to the making of the said telescope, & which I doubt not but will prove much more grateful then the communication of that instrument..."

In February he dispatched a lengthy letter, entitled "A Theory of Light and Colours." The response would confirm all his worst fears about engagement in the world of intellectual debates.

HAZARDOUS SUBSTANCES
A description of the process by which Newton created the alloy for the mirror highlights the dangers of home forging:

"The way, which he used, was this. He first melted the Copper alone, then put in the Arsenick, which being melted, he stirred them a little together, bewaring in the mean time, not to draw in breath near the pernicious fumes. After this, he put in Tin, and again so soon as that was melted (which was very suddenly) he stirred them well together, and immediately poured them off..."

"... examined here by some of the most eminent in optical science and practice, and applauded by them."

Hypothesis vs. Theory

WITH HIS LETTER TO THE
ROYAL SOCIETY, NEWTON
PROVED HIMSELF TO BE A
MAN AHEAD OF HIS TIME,
FOR "A THEORY OF LIGHT
AND COLORS" WAS MORE
THAN JUST AN ACCOUNT OF
BRILLIANT EXPERIMENTS AND
A NEW THEORY TO EXPLAIN
THEM—IT WAS A REVOLUTION
IN PHILOSOPHY, A NEW WAY OF
THINKING, THE BEGINNING OF
REAL SCIENCE, AND, IN THE
EYES OF MANY, THE FIRST
DEMONSTRATION OF THE ONE
TRUE PATH TO KNOWLEDGE
AND TRUTH.

Hot Topic

The distinction between hypothesis and theory is as important as ever, given the fierce debate over the teaching of evolution and attempts to promote a form of creationism known as "intelligent design" (ID). Critics of evolution argue that it should be taught as simply "one of several possible theories," by implication of equivalent status to ID. But the ID position is based on a fundamental misunderstanding of the meaning of the word "theory" in a scientific context. Were Newton alive today, he would be bitterly opposed to the strategy of the ID camp.

In his paper, Newton tried to make it clear from the start that he was not offering hypotheses: "For what I shall tell concerning them is not an Hypothesis but most rigid consequence, not conjectured by barely inferring tis thus because not otherwise ... but evinced by the mediation of experiments concluding directly & without suspicion of doubt." This distinction between hypothesis and speculation on the one hand, and experimental evidence that proves a theory on the other, is absolutely crucial to understanding what was revolutionary about Newton's approach and why he was so angry with the response to his paper.

Vain and Empty Speculation

One of the initial hostile responses was from a French Jesuit, Ignace Pardies, who simply asserted that Newton's "hypothesis" was mistaken, an objection calculated to rile the Cambridge man. Newton crushed these objections with ease, sniffily observing, "[I offer] nothing else than certain properties of light which, now discovered, I think are not difficult to prove, and which if I did not know to be true, I should prefer to reject as vain and empty speculation, than acknowledge them as my hypothesis."

But he met with similar objections from much more heavyweight detractors, Robert Hooke and Christiaan Huygens (see pages 66–8). They also tried to argue that Newton's paper proposed little more than hypotheses, as they themselves had done in their work, like almost everyone else up to this point. This, in turn, meant that his suggestions about the nature of light had only as much authority as he did; as more experienced, established natural philosophers, they may well have assumed that their authority outweighed his and that therefore their hypotheses were superior.

Fine Distinctions

But these objections were based on a misunderstanding about the nature of Newton's argument, and the fine distinction between a hypothesis and a theory. In everyday language these two words are largely interchangeable, but in scientific discourse there is a very important difference between them. A hypothesis is a speculation, perhaps based on insights and observations, even on experimental evidence—it may even be absolutely correct and accurate. But, crucially, it has not been proved: it is simply one possible explanation that is more or less plausible and more or less fits the facts.

A theory, on the other hand, is a set of propositions that has been tested and proved by observation and experiment, often backed up by mathematical proofs. Its truth does not depend on the experimenter; it can be independently verified by anyone. This is not to say that scientific theories are unassailable—if a new experiment or observation can be produced that clearly contradicts the theory, the theory must be modified or dumped, but until this happens the theory can arguably be said to be objectively true.

Hypotheses non Fingo

Newton grasped this while most of his contemporaries still clung to their pre-scientific ways of approaching the truth. It was a principle he would return to again and again, particularly in his masterwork the *Principia*, where he famously asserted, "Hypotheses non fingo" ("I frame no hypotheses" or "I do not feign hypotheses"):

"I frame no hypotheses; for whatever is not deduced from the phenomena is to be called an hypothesis; and hypotheses … have no place in experimental philosophy."

With this bold claim Newton was asserting his break with millennia of philosophical tradition and staking out a new path to truth, which has come to be the core of what is now known as the "scientific method."

Proponents of this system of thinking argue that it is the only route to objective truth. For Newton it served the dual purpose of lifting him above criticism, on the basis that he was offering only incontrovertible, irrefutable truths. Unfortunately critics persisted in disputing his findings, leading to years of bitter feuding.

"I frame no hypotheses; for whatever is not deduced from the phenomena is to be called an hypothesis"

Sir Francis Bacon (1561–1626), philosopher of science who championed the use of experiment and observation over speculation.

"God forbid we should give out a dream of our own imagination for a pattern of the world."

— SIR FRANCIS BACON

Exposed to the Light

UP UNTIL NOW NEWTON HAD LARGELY WORKED IN ISOLATION. HE HAD NEITHER THE EXPERIENCE NOR THE TEMPERAMENT FOR THE CUT AND THRUST OF INTELLECTUAL DISPUTE, STILL LESS THE DELICACIES OF POLITICS OR THE FINESSE OF DIPLOMACY. ABOVE ALL, HE WAS A MAN AHEAD OF HIS TIME. WHILE HE HAD MASTERED THE DISTINCTION BETWEEN HYPOTHESIS AND THEORY, HIS PEERS STILL HELD A PRE-SCIENTIFIC MINDSET. THE STAGE WAS SET FOR A TITANIC CLASH.

Newton's key adversary over the next four years and more would be Robert Hooke (1635–1703): The two had much in common. Hooke too lost his father at an early age, and had risen from relatively humble beginnings to distinguish himself by force of intellect. In personality, however, they were very different; Hooke was garrulous, boastful, extrovert: a gossip and intriguer. He enjoyed the life of the big city with its teeming coffee houses and convivial dinners; while Newton sat in glorious isolation, contemplating fundamental truths of mathematics and physics, Hooke's magpie intellect flitted between topics, from geology to anatomy, watchmaking to flying machines. His ingenuity at experiment had secured him the role of curator of experiments to the Royal Society.

Battle Lines

Hooke's magnum opus was his 1665 book *Micrographia*, a treatise on microscopy and also a consideration of the nature of light. He was a keen proponent of a wave theory of light, arguing that light existed as pressure waves or pulses in the ether. Though loath to admit it, Newton was a fan of the *Micrographia*, and had drawn much inspiration from it, but as a corpuscularian (one who thought light was composed of corpuscles, or particles) he opposed the wave theory. When "A Theory of Light and Colours" was read to the Royal Society, Hooke immediately felt his position to be under attack and launched a counter-assault:

One of the microscopes built by Hooke; he sold versions to wealthy amateur philosophers.

"I have perused the excellent discourse of Mr Newton … and I was not a little pleased with the niceness and curiosity of his observations. But although I wholly agree with him as to the truth of those he has alleged, as having by many hundreds of trials found them so, yet as to his hypothesis of solving the phenomenon of colours thereby I confess I cannot yet see any undeniable argument to convince me of the certainty thereof. For all the experiments & observations I have hitherto made, nay and even those very experiments which he alleged, do seem to me to prove that light is nothing but a pulse or motion propagated through an homogeneous, uniform and transparent medium."

In particular, Hooke disagreed with Newton's assertion that a prism merely separated out pre-existing colors, insisting that a prism adds color to light as an organ pipe or violin string adds sound to the air, and he flatly denied the conclusions Newton had drawn from the *experimentum crucis.*

"I wonder how Mr Hooke could imagine that when I had asserted the Theory with the greatest rigour, I should be so forgetful as afterwards to assert the fundamental supposition itself with no more than a perhaps."

A Little Troubled

Newton was furious. He objected that Hooke's criticism of the *experimentum crucis* was little more than "a bare denial without assigning a reason," and railed against his critic:

"I was a little troubled to find a person so much concerned for an Hypothesis, from whom in particular I most expected an unconcerned & indifferent examination... Mr Hooke thinks himself concerned to reprehend me... But he knows well that it is not for one man to prescribe Rules to the studies of another, especially not without understanding the grounds on which he proceeds."

Newton, however, had left himself open to attack with a line in his paper in which he asserted that "it can no longer be disputed ... whether light be a body," without really having the evidence to turn this from a hypothesis to a theory. Hooke had made much of this apparent slip, but Newton struck back, pointing out that his argument for the corpuscular theory of light was "at most but a very plausible consequence of the doctrine, and not a fundamental supposition," and that he had, in fact, been careful to use the word "perhaps."

The underside of a louse, a "description of a minute body made by magnifying glasses."

A plate from Hooke's Micrographia showing a louse.

Standing on the Shoulders of Giants

NEWTON DEMOLISHED ONE OBJECTION AFTER ANOTHER, BUT FOUND THE DISPUTES INCREASINGLY VEXATIOUS. AS SECRETARY OF THE ROYAL SOCIETY, IT WAS HENRY OLDENBURG'S JOB TO MEDIATE CORRESPONDENCE BETWEEN NEWTON AND THE OTHER FELLOWS. HE WAS RENOWNED FOR HIS POWERS OF TACT AND DIPLOMACY, AND FOUND HE NEEDED ALL OF THEM TO COPE WITH AN INCREASINGLY PETULANT NEWTON AS THE FEUD WITH HOOKE RUMBLED ON.

Newton had dealt with the initial round of Hooke's objections, and the curator of experiments had promised to perform his own versions of the *experimentum crucis* and the other trials in order to test the validity of Newton's work. But there was another source of objections who could not be so easily dismissed. Christiaan Huygens was one of the great minds of the Enlightenment, a Dutchman who had made important discoveries in astronomy, horology, optics, and mathematics. He too was a proponent of the wave theory of light, and like Hooke he objected to what he (mistakenly) understood to be Newton's hypothesizing.

Oldenburg passed a letter from Huygens on to Newton, who responded with a tantrum. "Sir I desire that you procure that I may be put out from being any longer a Fellow of the R. Society," he wrote back in March 1673. Although he did not make good on this threat, he wrote to Collins a month later to complain: "… I could wish I had met with no rudeness in some other things. And therefore I hope you will not think it strange if to prevent accidents of that nature for the future I decline that conversation which has occasioned what is past." Other matters concerned him now, for he was deeply engaged in alchemical and theological studies, and nothing more was heard from him for nearly three years.

*Christiaan Huygens
(1629-95)*

The Properties of Light

Finally, in December 1675, Newton was ready to re-engage with the Royal Society, sending two papers. "An Hypothesis Explaining the Properties of Light" actively embraced the term "hypothesis," setting forth speculations on the nature of light and matter. The second, "Discourse of Observations," detailed experiments in which he attempted to demonstrate his hypothesis. The papers included jibes at Hooke, whom he effectively accused of plagiarizing the French Jesuit Honoré Fabri. Hooke was incandescent, asserting that it was Newton who had plagiarized his *Micrographia*. Newton's response was magiste-

THE MAGNUS EFFECT

Newton's genius was profligate; he made discoveries almost casually. In 1672, watching fellows play tennis on the court at Trinity, he had noted a curious phenomenon in which a spinning ball would move through the air in a curve. His explanation— "Its parts on that side, where the motions conspire, must press and beat the contiguous Air more violently than on the other, and there excite a reluctancy and reaction of the Air proportionately greater"—must have been overlooked, for the same explanation was not "officially discovered" until 1852 by Heinrich Gustav Magnus.

rial. Far from replicating Hooke's researches, his own studies acted "to destroy all he has said"; he added tartly "I suppose he will allow me to make use of what I took the pains to find out."

Hooke decided to try another tactic, beginning a direct, private correspondence with his enemy. Convention dictated that such a correspondence be respectful in the extreme, and so the two exchanged honeyed words, culminating in February 1676 in Newton's apparently modest summation: "What Descartes did was a good step. You have added much several ways... If I have seen further it is by standing on the shoulders of Giants."

Some Newton scholars think that he was clearly aiming a cruel jibe at Hooke, described by the contemporary portraitist John Aubrey in his *Brief Lives* as "but of middling stature, something crooked, pale faced, and his face but little below, but his head is large." Others point out that Newton was not the original author of the phrase, and that the sentiment was a conventional one. Whether or not Hooke was offended, on April 27, 1676 he finally performed the long-awaited replication of Newton's *experimentum crucis* before the Society, marking an important milestone in the development of science. An experimental verification of a hypothesis had been replicated for the first time, properly elevating it to the status of theory.

However, in 1678 Oldenburg died and Hooke succeeded him as secretary. Newton withdrew from all correspondence, retreating into a period of isolation at Cambridge, delving ever deeper into nature's secrets by any means available.

Tennis in the 17th century was very different from the modern version; it was played with hard balls in enclosed courts.

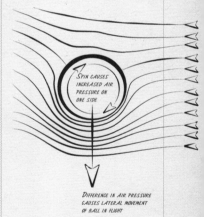

SPIN CAUSES INCREASED AIR PRESSURE ON ONE SIDE

DIFFERENCE IN AIR PRESSURE CAUSES LATERAL MOVEMENT OF BALL IN FLIGHT

The Magnus effect: spin increases speed of air flow on one side of ball, decreasing pressure due to Bernoulli's principle.

"If I have seen further it is by standing on the shoulders of Giants."

— IN A LETTER FROM NEWTON TO HOOKE, FEBRUARY 5, 1676

Solving the Crime of the Millennium

Newton was a deeply pious man. His Puritanism was both a comfort and a guide to him, and he saw the search for knowledge and truth as sacraments—discovering nature's secrets was a way to glorify God. The Bible was seen as being of equal importance to nature as a repository of God's wisdom and purpose, and to Newton theological research was as important as his scientific pursuits. The roots of his learning went deep; he had been reading theology since inheriting his step-father's books and studying in the library at St. Wulfram's in Grantham. In fact, four of the ten books he bought on arrival at Cambridge were theological works.

Ordination Deadline

In order to remain a fellow of Trinity (and by extension in order to remain Lucasian professor), Newton had a deadline by which he had to become an ordained minister of Anglican clergy—by

A grisly depiction of the Holy Trinity, with God the Father supporting the Son, while the Holy Ghost in the form of a dove perches on his shoulder.

1672 he had already been a fellow for four years and within the next three years he would be expected to take orders. Around this time he started a new notebook, with headings in his usual style, but according to Westfall: "While the list of headings appears unexceptionably orthodox, Newton's entries under them suggest that certain doctrines, which had the inherent capacity to draw him away from orthodoxy, had begun to fascinate him."

Over the next few years he pursued a massive program of reading in theology, but always with an eye to one issue: the nature of Christ and God. According to conventional doctrine, adopted in the early history of the Church, Christ and God (and the Holy Spirit) were one and the same, three in one, the Holy Trinity. But to Newton this assertion rang false on both logical grounds and the evidence of scripture; Christ might be more than human, but he could not be as fully divine as God.

The Ultimate Idolatry

The more he researched, the more he became convinced that a great fraud had been perpetrated to corrupt the legacy of the early Church, and that scripture itself had been corrupted to support Trinitarianism. Delving deep into the history of the Church and the development of scripture, he pinpointed the genesis of this corruption to the fourth century, and the triumph of Athanasius (a Trinitarian) over Arius (who denied the Trinity). Henceforth he would be a follower of the heresy known as Arianism, which denies the Trinity; in his eyes the conventional Catholic/Anglican doctrine in which Christ is worshiped as God was idolatry, the most fundamental sin.

If he was right, then the doctrine of transubstantiation and the practice of communion were horrific perversions. "If there be no transubstantiation never was Pagan idolatry so bad as the Romans [Catholic Church]," he wrote in the early 1670s. He felt that he had uncovered the crime of the millennium, and as Westfall comments: "It is not hard to understand why Newton became impatient with interruptions from minor diversions such as optics and mathematics. He had committed himself to a reinterpretation of the tradition central to the whole of European civilisation."

Athanasius (c.296–373), a key force in promulgating Trinitarian dogma who earned the title "father of orthodoxy."

"It was the son of God which he sent into the world & not a human soul that suffered for us. If there had been such a human soul in our Saviour, it would have been a thing of too great consequence to have been wholly omitted by the Apostles."

— From Newton's "Argumenta and Twelve Points on Arian Christology," c.1674

Arianism posed a huge problem for Newton's upcoming ordination, as part of which he would be forced to declare that he accepted the "Thirty Nine Articles of the Anglican Church," which include belief in the Trinity. In fact, he had already effectively done so four times—when he signed for his bachelor's degree in 1665 and his master's degree in 1668, received his fellowship in 1667 and his professorship in 1669—but now he was testing the limits of his conscience. In the event he dodged the bullet by gaining a royal dispensation from the king himself, probably thanks to the good offices of Isaac Barrow, the Royal Chaplain. He was exempted from taking holy orders and could retain the Lucasian chair. Now he was free to devote all his energies to the pursuit that obsessed him above all others: alchemy.

CHAPTER FOUR

PHILOSOPHER BY FIRE

Introducing Alchemy

ALCHEMY IS THE ART AND SCIENCE OF MATERIAL AND SPIRITUAL TRANSFORMATION. ITS MOST FAMOUS—OR INFAMOUS—GOALS ARE THE CREATION OF THE PHILOSOPHER'S STONE AND THE ELIXIR OF IMMORTALITY; BUT FOR MANY OF THE GREAT ADEPTS, AND NEWTON WAS ONE OF THEM, THESE WERE MERELY INCIDENTAL TO THE REDISCOVERY OF OCCULT KNOWLEDGE: A SYSTEM TO UNDERSTAND AND MANIPULATE NATURE THAT WAS KNOWN TO THE ANCIENTS BUT HAD BEEN LONG SINCE LOST.

Alchemy is best known as a sort of magical chemistry, the aim of which is to create a mythical substance known as the philosopher's stone, to which many wonderful powers and properties are ascribed, chief among them the ability to transmute the base metal lead into gold. The alchemist's other intent is said to be the concoction of the *elixir vitae*, the elixir of life, which conveys immortality upon the drinker.

To achieve these aims the alchemist mixed powders and potions, heating, dissolving, and distilling combinations of mercury, iron, acid, and a hundred other exotic chemicals in furnaces, crucibles, and alembics (glass or copper vessels). But rather than the language of chemistry, alchemy used a system of strange names and obscure symbols, allegory, and code. The alchemist worked in secret and shared his researches with a select few, initiates into the same world of occult knowledge.

A Brief History of Alchemy

Alchemy claims to trace its roots back to the dawn of civilization and beyond, and such claims of ancient lineage have been central to the alchemical project. The progenitors of alchemical knowledge are said to be figures such as Moses, Solomon, and the Hellenic-Egyptian gods Hermes and Isis. In fact, the set of practices that came to be known as alchemy most likely grew up in Alexandria in the period between the second and fourth centuries CE (a parallel, older tradition existed independently in China and India). Texts were written at this time that were

Thomas Aquinas wrote several treatises on alchemy and concluded that alchemically produced gold was morally equivalent to real gold.

later attributed to much more ancient sources, such as Hermes Trismegistus (Hermes the Thrice Great), a mythical demigod figure who combined attributes of Greek and Egyptian divinities and legendary heroes. The wisdom contained in these works became known as "hermetic." At least as important as the practical instructions, the hermetic tradition involved philosophical and spiritual secrets.

The alchemical tradition was adopted and expanded by the Islamic world, where it was preserved through the Dark Ages and fed back into Europe during the Middle Ages and Renaissance. Islamic alchemists picked up concepts such as the philosopher's stone and the elixir of life from Oriental sources and introduced them into the Western tradition. Many of the great scholars of Europe during the Medieval and Early Modern period, including Thomas Aquinas, Roger Bacon, Agrippa, Paracelsus, and Dee, were associated

Above: Arcane symbols for the chemical elements used by alchemists.

Right: A portrait of the alchemist Paracelsus from the 1567 book *Astronomica et Astrologica*.

with alchemy and said to be *magi*—masters of the occult arts. They were said to have created marvellous automata, to converse with spirits, or to have control over the weather by their alchemical arts.

By the 17th century there was an informal network of magi corresponding across Europe, swapping ideas and books, rumors and claims. As this network became self-conscious some termed it the Invisible College; others penned manifestos proclaiming the advent of a new brotherhood, the Rosicrucians. Scientific institutions such as the Royal Society traced their roots in part to these occult societies, and many of Newton's most illustrious contemporaries also engaged in alchemical research.

A Grovelling Delusion

There was also a tawdry, disreputable side to alchemy; the 19th-century historian Charles Mackay dismissed it as "a grovelling delusion." Not only was it associated with sorcery, a blasphemous and illegal practice, it had long been the refuge of charlatans and scoundrels—known as "puffers"—who used the promise of unlimited gold to deceive the unwary. Meanwhile, many practitioners had been led to ruin by their obsession, losing their fortunes and even their minds. Newton, however, saw himself as very different from a mere amateur "chymist."

"... the course of Nature ... seems delighted with transmutations." — NEWTON, *OPTICKS*, 1706

FOOL'S ERRAND

Newton was well aware that alchemy could be the graveyard of philosophers and a surefire route to ruin; writing to his friend John Locke in 1692, he described the unhappy fate of a group who thought they had secured a recipe for turning lead into gold:

"... I heard some years ago of a company, who were upon this work in London... I enquired after them, and learnt that two of them were since forced to other means of living; and a third, who was the chief artist, was run so far into debt that he had much ado to live; and by these circumstances, I understood that these gentlemen could not make the thing succeed."

The Sacred Quest

NEWTON CONSIDERED HIMSELF A "PHILOSOPHER BY FIRE," AS SERIOUS, PHILOSOPHICAL ALCHEMISTS WERE KNOWN. HIS ALCHEMY HAD LITTLE IN COMMON WITH THE BASE MATERIALISM OF THE TRANSMUTATION OF LEAD INTO GOLD OR THE SINISTER SEARCH FOR POWER, AND WAS WHOLLY DIFFERENT FROM THE GRUBBY GET-RICH-QUICK SCHEMES AND CHEAP PARLOR TRICKS OF THE "PUFFERS." INSTEAD IT WAS A NOBLE PURSUIT FOR THE PURE OF HEART, A QUEST FOR SACRED TRUTHS AND A MORE PERFECT KNOWLEDGE OF GOD'S WORKS.

A copy of a diagram of the Philosopher's Stone ("lapis philosophicus") made by Newton, annotated in typical alchemical fashion — astrological and magical symbols adorn the border of each circle, and they are labeled with attributes of gender and humor.

For Newton the true aim of alchemy was far from the self-serving pursuit of gold: it was the quest for ultimate truth, for knowledge that, according to the prevailing view of history, humankind had once possessed but which was now lost.

The *Prisca Sapientia*

Today the prevailing myth of knowledge is that humanity is progressing, and that the history of knowledge is one of continual advancement. In Newton's day it was the opposite: it was generally believed that the earliest civilization, being closest to God, had also been the most perfect, complete with the most perfect wisdom. This original, perfect wisdom was known as the *prisca sapientia*, the pristine or primal wisdom, possessed by the ancients but since lost during humanity's long fall from grace down through the ages.

It was believed, however, that the secrets of the *prisca sapientia* were still accessible, encoded in the natural world for those who could penetrate their mysteries. According to John Maynard Keynes, Newton "regarded the universe as a cryptogram set by the Almighty"; through alchemy he would attempt to decode it.

God Complex

Many men had already tried. Through his voluminous reading Newton would have been aware of the efforts of previous magi, each believing he had come close to achieving the dream, encoding hints and clues in a dense allegorical language that ultimately recorded only their failures. Now he would take up the baton, launching himself into a quest that appealed to his vanity and ambition.

Where generations of the greatest minds had failed, he would succeed, for he saw

Femina melancholia

Femina melancholia

Femina phlegmatica

Femina phlegmatica

Masculina cholerica

Masculina sanguinia

Masculina sanguinia

himself in a special light. He believed this task was ordained to him by God and called it "the duty of the first moment." Possibly he believed it was no coincidence that he had been born on Christmas Day, and the extent of his vanity can perhaps be glimpsed in the pseudonym under which he chose to write alchemical treatises: Jeova Sanctus Unus, an anagram of the Latinized version of his name, which translates as "One Holy God."

Much of the equipment of the modern chemistry laboratory derives from the Medieval and Early Modern alchemists, who created flasks, beakers, alembics, and crucibles to aid their investigations.

The Pure of Heart

Newton believed himself fitted for the task for other reasons. He saw alchemy as a virtuous and noble endeavor: "a philosophy ... which tends ... to profit and to edification ... the scope [of which] is to glorify God, to teach a man how to live well..." —an undertaking that could only be successfully made by the righteous and incorruptible. To be successful the alchemist must have pure intentions, undergo a program of physical and spiritual purification (which might extend to diet, prayer, and ablutions), and be willing to undertake rigorous and lengthy experimental procedures. As a pious, abstemious man, almost certainly a virgin, with an unparalleled capacity for intense concentration and devotion to experiment, Newton was perhaps the perfect candidate for initiation into the Invisible College of alchemical adepts.

"They who search after the Philosophers' Stone are by their own rules obliged to a strict and religious life. That study is fruitful of experiments."

— NEWTON TO JOHN CONDUITT

Newton's Initiation

NEWTON'S INTEREST IN CHEMISTRY CAN REASONABLY BE TRACED BACK TO HIS CHILDHOOD FASCINATION WITH DYES AND COLORS, AND HIS ADOLESCENT APPRENTICESHIP AT THE APOTHECARY'S. BUT ALCHEMY WAS A DIFFERENT ORDER OF PURSUIT, AND HE OWED HIS INITIATION INTO ITS ARCANE LORE TO A NUMBER OF IMPORTANT MENTORS, WHO WOULD EVENTUALLY INTRODUCE HIM TO A SECRET SOCIETY OF SORTS, THE SHADOWY HARTLIB CIRCLE.

Newton's juvenile notebooks testify to his early facility with recipes and formulae, from the instructions for dyes and remedies that he copied from Bate, to the more sophisticated formulae he picked up working with Clark, the Grantham apothecary. But his introduction to chemistry of a different kind was probably down to Humphrey Babington, Clark's brother-in-law, and Henry More, a King's School alumnus who had gone on to become a leading natural philosopher at Cambridge and a noted alchemist. Newton probably came to the attention of this Grantham-Cambridge "intellectual mafia" thanks to his prodigious brilliance as a schoolboy; presumably they quickly perceived that here was a young man with the gifts and inclinations to go a long way in the pursuit of secret knowledge. At Cambridge Newton's tutelage in the occult arts continued, as he came under the influence of Isaac Barrow, another adept.

A Chymical Glossary

Newton approached alchemy much as he approached other subjects. He began by reading widely, and by interrogating what he read by making headings and taking notes. As early as 1666 he began to compile a glossary of chemical terms, inspired by Robert Boyle's *The Sceptical Chymist*, a groundbreaking book that began the work of putting chemistry, such as it was, on a more scientific basis. Boyle, a founder member of the Royal Society and leading proponent of the new experimental philosophy, was a great influence on the young Newton, in terms of both science and alchemy. They met in 1675 and became friends and colleagues. Among the conventional headings, such as "Amalgam," "Crucible," and "Extraction," alchemical ones crept in: "menstruum peracutum," for instance, was a recipe of Boyle's for a substance that would dissolve gold. Many of these alchemical entries were just headings; perhaps Newton was conscious that he was infringing on controversial territory and did not care to leave a paper trail. Later entries in the glossary were more bold: "Of the work with common gold."

Robert Boyle (1627–91), alchemist, pioneering experimentalist, and one of the founding fathers of the Royal Society, was a profound influence on Newton.

The Hartlib Circle

From 1668 to the late 1670s there are a number of episodes in Newton's life that remain unexplained. He made numerous visits to London, but who he visited and why was not recorded. He also spent time with unnamed "friends" in the country.

Newton is known to have received a regular flow of alchemical manuscripts, although their source is a mystery; notes he made on some of them use cryptic initials, such as "Mr F." This mysterious "Mr F." is believed to have been Ezekiel Foxcroft, an alchemist and, like Boyle, an associate of the Hartlib Circle, a loose group of alchemical inquirers that had grown up around Samuel Hartlib, a Polish Prussian who had passed away by the time Newton began to practice alchemy.

The Hartlib Circle attempted to combine the magical approach of alchemy with the rational approach of the new mechanical philosophy of Descartes and others. Boyle's 1666 book *The Origine of Formes and Qualities*, was a distillation of these efforts, eagerly devoured by Newton.

It seems likely that Newton was, at least informally, inducted into the Hartlib Circle and spent time with its members, imbibing concepts that would play a significant part in the formation of his theories about gravity and other laws of physics. It was Newton who would eventually accomplish the Hartlib Circle's goal of marrying alchemy and science.

SELF-DOSING

When it came to concocting his formulae, Newton maintained a penchant for self-medication (and a concomitant degree of hypochondria). His long-time roommate Wickins recalled that, "He sometime suspected Himself to be inclining to a Consumption, & the Medicine He made use of was the Lucatellus Balsam which when he had compos'd Himself, He would now & then melt in Quantity about a Quarter of a Pint & so drink it."

"Collected out of a M.S. communicated to Mr F. by W.S. 1670, & by Mr F. to me 1675."

— CRYPTIC NOTES THAT NEWTON INSCRIBED ON AN ALCHEMICAL MANUSCRIPT CALLED "MANNA"

In the Laboratory

ONCE A FIRE WAS LIT WITHIN NEWTON'S BREAST IT BURNED BRIGHTLY. HE PLUNGED INTO ALCHEMICAL LABORS—FIRST READING AND MAKING NOTES, AND THEN, FROM AROUND 1669, ENTERING A PERIOD OF ACTIVE EXPERIMENTATION. HE SET UP A LABORATORY IN HIS ROOMS AT CAMBRIDGE, AND WITH FIRST JOHN WICKINS AND LATER HUMPHREY NEWTON AS ASSISTANTS, HE TOILED LONG HOURS OVER THE CRUCIBLE AND THE ALEMBIC.

Newton was no mere dabbler. He threw himself wholeheartedly into the sacred work of alchemy, risking his health and even his sanity. When he wrote impatiently to those wishing to dispute with him the details of his optics or some other piece of natural philosophy, it was because his whole attention was focused on this arcane labor. According to Betty Jo Teeter Dobbs, the pre-eminent scholar of Newton's alchemy, "each brief and often abruptly cryptic laboratory report hides behind itself untold hours with hand-built furnaces of brick, with crucible, with mortar and pestle, with the apparatus of distillation, and with charcoal fires: experimental sequences sometimes ran for weeks, months, or even years."

Tooled Up

In 1669 Newton made his first visit to London, primarily for the purpose of equipping himself for the alchemical project ahead. He made contact with booksellers and purchased several works on alchemy: the seeds of a mighty collection. Of the great library of books in his possession when he died, 169 were works on alchemy and chemistry, and according to Michael White, author of the biography *Isaac Newton: The Last Sorcerer*, "it has been said that Newton possessed the finest and most extensive collection of alchemical texts ever accumulated up to his day."

Lab Rats

At first Newton set up a laboratory in the rooms that he and Wickins shared. In 1673 the two moved to new rooms, to which was attached a sort of shed, and Newton requisitioned this for a dedicated alchemical laboratory. His later assistant Humphrey Newton described it: "On the left end of the Garden, was his Elaboratory, near the East end of the Chappell, where he, at these sett Times, employ'd himself in, with a great deal of satisfaction & Delight." The laboratory, he recalled, "... was well furnished with chymical Materials, as Bodyes, Receivers, ffends, Crucibles &c, which was made very little use of, the Crucibles excepted, in which he [fused] his Metals: He would sometimes, thô very seldom, look into an old mouldy Book, which lay in his Elaboratory, I think it was titled, – *Agricola de*

"... he aim'd at somthing beyond the Reach of humane Art & Industry."

— HUMPHREY NEWTON

NEWTON

PREMATURELY GRAY

Newton was noted for his hair, which he often wore bare (without a wig), and which was gray from an early age. The son of his erstwhile roommate and lab assistant Wickins recalled: "He was turning Grey, I think, at Thirty, and when my Father observed that to him as the Effect of his deep attention of Mind; He would jest with the Experiments he made so often with Quick Silver as if from thence he took so soon that Colour." In practice the use of quicksilver (mercury) was no jesting matter, as Newton would discover to his cost.

Newton pictured in later life, wigless, as he often was in his youth.

Metallis, The transmuting of Metals, being his Chief Design, for which Purpose Antimony was a great Ingredient."

Humphrey Newton was especially struck by the relentless nature of his master's labors, reporting that "He very rarely went to Bed, till 2 or 3 of the clock, sometimes not till 5 or 6, lying about 4 or 5 hours, especially at spring & ffall of the Leaf, at which Times he us'd to imploy about 6 weeks in his Elaboratory, the ffire scarcely going out either Night or Day, he siting up one Night, as I did another till he had finished his Chymical Experiments, in the Performances of which he was the most accurate, strict, exact: What his Aim might be, I was not able to penetrate into but his Paine, his Diligence at those sett times, made me think, he aim'd at somthing beyond the Reach of humane Art & Industry."

Through diligent research Newton became something of an expert on the design and construction of furnaces.

The Scientific Magus

ONCE AGAIN NEWTON TURNED TO HIS NOTEBOOKS, WHICH REPRESENTED A SORT OF EXTERNALIZATION OF HIS MASSIVE INTELLECT, ALLOWING HIM TO ARRANGE HIS THINKING AND CONCEPTUALIZE THE BIGGER PICTURE—ALWAYS HE WAS SEARCHING FOR THE UNIFYING PRINCIPLES, THE UNDERLYING LAWS. ALCHEMY WAS NO DIFFERENT, EXCEPT THAT HE CONCEALED HIS INTERESTS BY WRITING IN CODE, A CODE THAT HAS ONLY RECENTLY BEEN DECIPHERED.

Until relatively recently Newton's pursuit of alchemy has been regarded as an embarrassment, a stain on his reputation as the first and prototypical scientist, and with good reason, for the practice of alchemy had essential characteristics that seem to place it fundamentally at odds with science and with Newton's lifelong project. It was based on a priori assumptions and rules (in other words, statements and propositions held to be true, even though they had not been tested or proved; for example, the assumption that there were four basic elements, or the belief that there existed correspondences between metals and signs of the zodiac). Alchemical procedures, techniques, and experiments (if they can be called that) stressed subjective variables, such as the mental and spiritual state of the experimenter, so that it was believed an experiment might fail because the experimenter was not sufficiently pure of spirit, for instance. According to Michael White, "it is this concept, more than any other, which distinguishes alchemy from the orthodox chemistry that superseded it."

Rather than sharing results and the details of experiments, such as techniques and quantities, so that others could examine, critique, and replicate, as in science, alchemists believed in hiding results and techniques through allegory and encryption. In fact, alchemical tracts emphasized the opposite of replicability, stressing the individualism of experimenter and experiments. Finally, alchemists resisted attempts to formalize their art or bring knowledge together into coherent systems or theories.

No Ordinary Alchemist

But Newton was no ordinary alchemist. He approached the "Work" differently, making careful notes of his experiments, attempting to synthesize his massive reading in order to produce axioms. In the words of Westfall: "Always striving to extract the general from the specific, Newton set out at once to reduce the multitudinous testimony of his reading to the one true process." He drew up a list of 47 axioms of alchemy, with references. He collected allegories and images that represented the same substance or process; sometimes he would list up to

"Concerning Magnesia or the green Lion. It is called Prometheus & the Chameleon. Also Androgyne, and virgin verdant earth in which the Sun has never cast its rays although he is its father and the moon its mother..." — FROM NEWTON'S "INDEX CHEMICUS," C.1680

50 different descriptions. Eventually, the "unscientific" language of alchemy would provide him with the conceptual basis to construct the ultimate scientific model of nature.

In the meantime, however, he was happy to employ that language, with the result that his alchemical writings today present an enigmatic jumble of colorful jargon and allegory. For instance, in one passage Newton describes "a wondrous bright water in which the sun doth set"; decoded, this refers to the use of a type of mercury ("bright water") to dissolve gold ("the sun"), the first step in a formula for the creation of the fabled philosopher's stone.

Things He Lost in the Fire

A major blow to his researches occurred in the winter of 1677–8, when a fire broke out in the laboratory as Newton made a rare visit to the college chapel. Although the laboratory was not completely destroyed, a number of papers he had been working on were lost. According to Stukeley, one of the lost works was nothing less than a *Principia Chemicum*, in which Newton was "explaining the principles of that mysterious art upon experimental and mathematical proofs and he valued it much, but it was unluckily burnt in his laboratory which casually took fire. He would never undertake that work again, a loss much to be regretted."

Other authorities argue that the lost work was an early version of *Opticks*, although Humphrey Newton was not convinced: "As for his *Opticks* being burnt, I know Nothing of it, but as I had heard from Others, That Accident happening before he writ his *Principia*."

"a wondrous bright water in which the sun doth set"

An imagining of the scene in Newton's study in the winter of 1677, when he lost important papers to a fire.

In Search of the Star Regulus

WITH HIS ASSISTANT WICKINS HEFTING HEAVY "KETTLES," STOKING THE FURNACES, AND TAKING NOTES, NEWTON SET TO WORK EXPLORING THE CHEMISTRY OF MERCURY, FAVORITE SUBSTANCE OF THE ALCHEMIST. BUT THIS WORK WOULD ULTIMATELY PROVE TO BE DISAPPOINTING, AND IT WAS WITH A DIFFERENT METAL, ANTIMONY, IN A RARE CRYSTALLIZED FORM KNOWN AS THE "STAR REGULUS," THAT HE ACHIEVED GREATER SUCCESS.

From Aristotle, alchemists had developed the theory that all matter was composed of four basic elements in differing proportions, and that by altering these proportions substances could be transmuted. Newton, who favored the atomic theory, argued against the doctrine of the Aristotelian elements, but he shared the basic belief in the possibility of transmutation, writing that "the Course of Nature ... seems delighted with Transmutations."

The First Matter

The most marvelously mutable substance of all was mercury or quicksilver, which the alchemists regarded as having near-magical properties. The only metal that was liquid at room temperature, it could dissolve gold, which could then be recovered later. Newton outlined its changeable nature:

"Mercury appears sometimes in the form of a hard, brittle Metal, sometimes in the form of a tasteless, pellucid, volatile white Earth, call'd Mercurius Dulcis; or in that of a red or white Precipitate, or in that of a fluid Salt; and in the Distillation it turns into Vapour, and being agitated in Vacuo, it shines like Fire. And after all these Changes it returns again into its first form of Mercury."

As an alchemist, Newton viewed mercury as the *prima materia*, the first matter—the essence or soul of matter, which had to be released by purging away the dross. He worked tirelessly to achieve this, hoping to make "sophic" or "philosopher's mercury," a special, mystical form of the substance essential to the manufacture of the philosopher's stone.

Newton took Boyle's experiments with mercury as his starting point. In 1692, for instance, he wrote to his friend and fellow alchemist John Locke:

"In the margin of [Boyle's] recipe was noted, that the mercury of the first work would grow hot with gold, and thence I gather that this recipe was the foundation of what he published many years ago, about such mercuries as would grow hot with gold... This satisfied me that mercury, by this recipe, may be brought to change its colours and properties, but not that gold may be multiplied thereby..."

He dissolved mercury in nitric acid and added lead filings. He mixed acid, mercury, and tin. Adding copper, he produced a blue solution. He heated, distilled, and precipitated. Always he would arrive back where he started, with a silver metallic precipitate that, on testing, proved to be nothing more than unaltered mercury. It was clear to Newton that he was simply making compounds of mercury and then recovering the ordinary metal. Disappointed, he turned to a new goal.

The symbol for Mercury, most important and mysterious of alchemical substances.

III. CLAVIS.

A print from a book by Basilius Valentinus. Creatures such as these were allegorical symbols of alchemical substances and processes.

The Regulus of Mars

Newton's next target was the manufacture of a crystalline compound called a "regulus," from the Latin for "little king." A regulus of the metal antimony, compounded with iron, produced a crystal with shards that radiated out from a central spot, and which was termed the Star Regulus or the Regulus of Mars. Newton knew from his reading that this was a powerful tool; for instance, according to the 15th-century alchemist Basilius Valentinus: "This Star is not so precious as to contain the Great [Philosopher's] Stone; but yet there is hidden in it a wonderful medicine."

Newton's notes reveal that he brought the same rigorous and systematic approach to this task as to all his endeavors, and he quickly succeeded in producing fine reguli. Their distinctive shapes, with lines radiating out from the center, would influence and inspire his greatest achievements in natural philosophy.

"If any reguli swell much in the midst of the upper surface it argues too much antimony if it be flat it argues too little. The better your proportions are the brighter and brittler will the Reg[ulus] be and the darker the scoria [intermediate stage] & the easier will they part... The work succeeds best in least quantities. If there be stuff like pitch long in cooling tis no good sign & often argues too much Antimony..."

— NEWTON'S ESSAY ON THE PRODUCTION OF REGULI OF ANTIMONY, c.1670

Active Principles

OF PARTICULAR INTEREST TO NEWTON WAS THE ESOTERIC CONCEPT OF "ACTIVE PRINCIPLES," MYSTIC FORCES THAT CONNECTED THE SPIRITUAL AND MATERIAL WORLDS, DROVE THE REACTIONS THAT ALCHEMISTS OBSERVED IN THEIR FLASKS AND CRUCIBLES, AND EVEN ANIMATED LIFE ITSELF. FOR NEWTON, ACTIVE PRINCIPLES WOULD COME TO OFFER A WAY TO BRIDGE THE GAP BETWEEN THE PHENOMENA HE OBSERVED IN HIS LABORATORY AND THOSE HE SAW THROUGH HIS TELESCOPE.

Production of the Regulus of Mars was just a starting point for Newton. According to one of his favorite alchemical authorities, Eirenaeus Philalethes ("Peaceful Lover of Truth"), the pseudonym of American writer George Starkey, the Star Regulus could be used to create sophic mercury by fusing it with silver or copper and then amalgamating it with mercury, producing a liquid in which gold could be dissolved and then recrystallized as "vegetation": branching, tree-like crystals.

Today this phenomenon is understood as the growth of purely mineral forms, as crystals in a saturated solution form more easily on the surface of existing crystals, but it has an unmistakeably organic semblance. Observing this peculiar phenomenon take place in his laboratory must have made a powerful impression on Newton, for here, in action, was the secret spirit he had been reading about.

Universal Spirit

For alchemists, mere matter was of limited interest. They believed that the material world was animated by a mystical spirit force, sometimes called the "Universal Spirit." This force, perhaps divine in origin, was able to act upon matter without being itself altered. It was behind all forms of activity in nature, from the reaction of chemicals in a crucible to the germination of seeds and the birth of animals. Newton called it "vegetative" because of the plant-like behavior it could induce in minerals, and according to Betty Jo Teeter Dobbs: "Newton was concerned from the first in his alchemical work to find evidence for the existence of a vegetative principle operating in the natural world, a principle that he understood to be the secret, universal, animating spirit of which the alchemists spoke."

Jupiter enthroned, after a sketch by Newton's own hand.

Vegetable Action

Around 1672 Newton penned an alchemical tract that was entitled "Of Natures Obvious Laws & Processes in Vegetation," and set out his conception of vegetable action as a unifying force: "That vegetation is the sole effect of a latent spirit & that this spirit is the same in all things." As he explored the

"There is therefore ... in the textures of the grosser matter a more subtle secret & noble way of working in all vegetation..."

idea further, he began to conceive of an invisible force extending simultaneously throughout a whole mass:

"There is therefore ... in the textures of the grosser matter a more subtle secret & noble way of working in all vegetation ... & the immediate seat of these operations is not the whole bulk of matter, but rather an exceeding subtle & unimaginably small portion of matter diffused through the mass which if it separated there would remain but a dead & inactive earth."

Active Principles and Gravity

In time this notion would mature to provide Newton with the conceptual basis to explain gravity, a force which, he argued, acted at a distance without any material or corporeal intermediary, yet extended simultaneously throughout and between bodies. Compare the passage above with one from the *Principia*, in which he hints at the alchemical source of his theories about gravity as a force acting at a distance, and also perhaps alludes to some sort of unified theory of matter and energy, gravity and electromagnetism:

VISION OF THE FUTURE
On one of his alchemical manuscripts Newton sketched an allegorical figure of Jupiter enthroned (opposite), with lines of mystic force coming from celestial orbs at his fingers to planets, representing the elements, at his feet. Did this prefigure his conception of gravity as an occult force acting at a distance?

"And now we might add something concerning a certain most subtle Spirit which pervades and lies hid in all gross bodies; by the force and action of which Spirit the particles of bodies mutually attract one another at near distances, and cohere, if contiguous; and electric bodies operate to greater distances, as well repelling as attracting the neighbouring corpuscles; and light is emitted, reflected, refracted, inflected, and heats bodies... But these are things that cannot be explained in few words, nor are we furnished with that sufficiency of experiments which is required to an accurate determination and demonstration of the laws by which this electric and elastic Spirit operates."

Clavis and Praxis

NEWTON'S PURSUIT OF ALCHEMY HAD HELPED LEAD HIM TO HIS GREATEST SCIENTIFIC ACHIEVEMENT, ALTHOUGH THE DEBT WOULD NOT BE ACKNOWLEDGED FOR CENTURIES. AS HE FOCUSED HIS ENERGIES ONCE MORE ON NATURAL PHILOSOPHY, DID HIS OCCULT PURSUITS FALL BY THE WAYSIDE? IN FACT, NEWTON DID NOT ABANDON THEM, AND WAS STILL EXPERIMENTING AND READING INTO THE 1690s, WHEN HE ENTERED HIS TIME OF CRISIS.

In alchemy Newton's genius for analysis and synthesis—for collecting data, assembling it into a whole, and abstracting from it principles, patterns, and laws—faced its sternest test, for here was a field of dead ends and blind alleys, contradictory codes and illusory promise. One of his first efforts to pull together what he had learned was a manuscript he titled "Clavis," or "The Key," written in 1675, which gives detailed instructions on how to make philosophic mercury. "Clavis" demonstrates how Newton was attempting to approach this magical topic in scientific fashion, with detailed description of laboratory procedures, including precise quantities, so that any reader could replicate the experiments.

In around 1680 he began to compile what he called an "Index Chemicus," which would systematize his massive reading by collecting under 115 headings references from every alchemical work he had studied. But this disorderly field would not submit to his discipline; the list grew to 251. He pruned it and began again; eventually it swelled to 714 headings.

Making Jupiter Fly

Time and again there were false dawns. In the spring of 1681 Newton thought he had reached a climax with his experiments; for instance, noting in his laboratory notebook (in typical allegorical code): "May 10 1681 I understood that the morning star is Venus and that she is the daughter of Saturn and one of the doves... May 18 I perfected the ideal solution. That is, two equal salts carry up Saturn." Yet these discoveries came to little. Three years later another apparent breakthrough: "May 23 [1684] I made Jupiter fly on his eagle." Yet this too seemed to lead nowhere.

Eventually Newton's alchemical studies came more into line with his natural philosophy, leading him to investigations of the properties of air and the nature of the ether, and to consideration of the active principles governing attraction and repulsion of bodies, a line of inquiry that would shortly bear fruit in his theory of gravity. After a period where Newton had been relatively absent from the theater of natural philosophy, the entreaties of others, and his own unquenchable curiosity, would lead him to take center stage once more.

Since ancient times the planet Jupiter has been imbued with mystical symbolism. Within the sphere of alchemy it represented the element tin.

Multiplication

Newton's interest in alchemy did not end here, however, although it did somewhat peter out. In a letter to John Locke in 1692, for instance, he expressed far more skepticism about one of the central ambitions of alchemy—"multiplication," or the creation of gold—than he had hitherto done: "In dissuading you from too hasty a trial of this recipe, I have forborne to say anything against multiplication in general, because you seem so persuaded of it; though there is one argument against it, which I could never find an answer to, and which, if you will let me have your opinion about it, I will send you in my next."

The following year, 1693, in the midst of a period of great mental and emotional turmoil (see pages 116–17), Newton's alchemical labors came to a head as he tried to compose a summation of his long years of study and experimentation in a document entitled "Praxis" ("Putting into action"), which Dobbs calls his "climactic composition in alchemy." The stress of this period seems to find its echo on the page, for the work was either a cipher within a cipher, or, as Newton biographer Michael White has it, "little more than a blend of naked delirium and false conviction – the work of a man on the edge of madness."

Amid typical impenetrable allegories—"Artefius tells us his fire dissolves & gives life to stones, & Pontanus that their fire is not transmuted with their matter, but turns it with all its faeces into the elixir."—Newton claimed to have achieved multiplication:

"Thus you may multiply each stone 4 times & no more for they will then become oils shining in the dark and fir for magical uses. You may ferment it with gold by keeping them in fusion for a day, & then project upon metals. This is the multiplication... Every multiplication will increase its virtue ten times &, if you use the mercury ... perhaps a thousand times. Thus you may multiply to infinity."

Of course this was nonsense, and Newton would soon be engaged in a massive project to prevent illegal "multiplication" as the master of the nation's money supply.

An alchemical depiction of the "man in the moon." Allegorical pictures and language helped alchemists preserve their secrets for the initiated alone.

"Artefius tells us his fire dissolves & gives life to stones, & Pontanus that their fire is not transmuted with their matter, but turns it with all its faeces into the elixir."

CHAPTER FIVE

GRAND DESIGNS: NEWTON'S *PRINCIPIA*

A Time of Departures

THE END OF THE **1670s** BROUGHT LOSS AND ISOLATION FOR NEWTON. HIS MOTHER TOOK ILL AND DIED, DESPITE HIS DESPERATE ATTEMPTS TO SAVE HER, WHILE HIS RELATIONSHIP WITH HIS LONGTIME ROOMMATE, JOHN WICKINS, APPEARS TO HAVE DISINTEGRATED AROUND THIS TIME. HOW DID NEWTON HANDLE THESE CRISES, AND WHAT EFFECT DID THEY HAVE ON HIS BRITTLE PSYCHOLOGY?

In May 1679 Newton received bad news from Woolsthorpe; his mother was seriously ill. Her youngest son, Benjamin, had caught a fever, and although Hannah had nursed him out of danger she had contracted the contagion. Newton was greeted with the news on his return from a nine-day sojourn in London; he set off immediately, not even delaying to sign out of the college register.

Newton the Physician

Arriving at Woolsthorpe, Newton personally took charge of his mother's treatment. He brought to bear all his experience of remedies and medicines, perhaps even imagining that his alchemical researches might offer some secret elixir that held mystical curative properties. "He sat up whole nights with her, gave her all her physic [medicine] himself, dressed all her blisters with his own hands, & made use of that manual dexterity for which he was so remarkable," related John Conduitt many years later. It was to no avail, for she died a few days later and was buried at the parish church of Colsterworth, where the register noted, "Mrs Hannah Smith... Was buried in woolen June the 4th 1679." She was recorded as the widow of Barnabas Smith, but was buried in the churchyard next to her first husband, Isaac Senior, presumably at the behest of her son, perhaps seeking to gain a last, hollow victory over his despised stepfather.

Newton inherited the not inconsiderable estate of his mother. Aged 37, he was now a wealthy gentleman scholar. He spent the next few months in Woolsthorpe arranging his affairs and managing the transition of the estate to new tenants, staying for long enough to oversee the cultivation of the crops and the autumn harvest. Material wealth had never been a great issue for him, but Newton was conscientious and exacting, hating to be ill-used. In putting the estate in order he found there were a number of outstanding debts to pursue, and set about it with a will. One of the debtors was one Edward Storer, the stepson of Clark the apothecary who had been his childhood roommate; this debt was settled without fuss. But a Mr. Todd, who owed the hefty sum of £100, received less leeway: "About your pretences of the moneys being ready long since & of a judgement which

The church at Colsterworth where Newton ensured that his mother was buried alongside his father, Isaac Sr., and not the hated Barnabas Smith.

you would have me believe I had against you I do not think it material to expostulate. I shall only tell you in general that I understand your way & therefore sue you. And if you intend to be put to no further charges you must be quick in payment for I intend to lose no time. I desire you therefore to pay it my sister Mary Pilkington at Market Overton as soon as you can & take her acquittance for your discharge."

Things Left Unsaid

There is little record of the psychological impact of the death of his mother, the woman whose initial abandonment in his infancy had occasioned so much neurosis and dysfunction. How did he feel when he was unable to save her, despite his personal attentions, his great learning and secret knowledge? His state of mind cannot have been improved by another significant departure from his life, that of John Wickins.

Wickins had been his roommate, assistant and sole companion for long stretches of time, but by 1679 he was spending more and more time away from the university. He left for good in 1683, and, apart from some cursory correspondence over a gift of Bibles 30 years later, the two men had no further communication for the rest of their lives. Had they parted acrimoniously? The true nature of their relationship remains a mystery; even after Newton became one of the greatest celebrities in Europe, Wickins had virtually nothing to say on the topic of their long association. Some biographers have read into this silence the unspoken tale of a romance gone sour, or perhaps a passion thwarted.

"I am glad to hear of your good health, & wish it may long continue, I remain ... Newton"

— **Letter to John Wickins after 30 years without contact, displaying an unmistakable chilliness**

Newton prepared poultices, dressings and medicines with his own hands, using the skills he had learned as an apothecary's apprentice.

Journey to the Center of the Earth

**IN 1679 NEWTON WAS
"CUMBRED WITH CONCERNS":
HIS MOTHER'S DEATH, THE
ESTATE AT WOOLSTHORPE,
THE END OF HIS RELATIONSHIP
WITH WICKINS, HIS OBSESSION
WITH ALCHEMY. YET HIS
NEMESIS HOOKE PERSISTED IN
ATTEMPTING TO ENGAGE HIM
IN PHILOSOPHICAL PURSUITS,
AND DESPITE HIMSELF NEWTON
FOUND HIMSELF DRAWN INTO
YET ANOTHER BATTLE, OVER
A THOUGHT EXPERIMENT THAT
WOULD SET HIM ON THE ROAD
TO THE *PRINCIPIA*.**

In November 1679 Newton finally returned from Woolsthorpe to his chambers at Trinity. Waiting for him was a letter from Robert Hooke, now secretary of the Royal Society. Perhaps mindful of his responsibility to engage with one of the brightest minds in England, Hooke's intent was to mollify:

"Difference in opinion if such there be me thinks should not be the occasion of Enmity." He offered up for consideration his own system of the world, published five years earlier; a detailed hypothesis of how the universe operated that appeared to anticipate Newton's famous achievements in the *Principia*.

Hooke proposed that the orbits of the planets around the Sun could be explained by "an attractive motion towards the central body" pulling them away from the straight-line motion they would otherwise follow. This theory predated Newton's *Principia* by a decade, so why is it not Hooke who is celebrated as the discoverer of gravity? The essential difference is that between a speculation and a demonstration. In essence, Hooke was making informed and inspired guesses about how the universe might work; Newton would show exactly how it did work, and he would prove it mathematically.

A Fancy of My Own

Newton attempted to brush the correspondence aside, replying later the same month:

"…heartily sorry I am that I am at present unfurnished with matter answerable to your expectations. For I have been this last half year in Lincolnshire cumbred with concerns… I have had no time to entertain Philosophical meditations… And before that, I had for some years past been endeavoured to bend my self from Philosophy … which makes me almost wholly unacquainted with what Philosophers at London or abroad have lately been employed about… I am almost as little

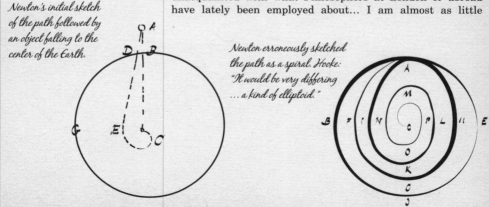

Newton's initial sketch of the path followed by an object falling to the center of the Earth.

Newton erroneously sketched the path as a spiral. Hooke: "It would be very differing … a kind of elliptoid."

concerned about it as one tradesman uses to be about another man's trade or a country man about learning."

But he did offer something in return: "a fancy of my own, about discovering the Earth's diurnal motion"—the spinning of the Earth on its axis. Many insisted that if it the Earth truly did spin then an object dropped from a tower should land to the west, the globe having spun beneath it. Newton suggested that in fact the object would be moving faster (being further out from the center of the planet than the surface) and would therefore drop to the east. He also sketched out the path it would follow if it could fall to the center of the Earth without resistance: a circular spiral.

> *"Hooke's correcting my spiral occasioned my finding the theorem by which I afterwards examined the ellipses."*

A Problem Framed

In fact, the theories about gravity held by both himself and Hooke meant that this was wrong—such an object should follow an elliptical path. Hooke seized upon the error and the ensuing spat once more drove Newton to distraction; but, in fact, the dispute prompted him to consider once more the issue of orbital mechanics, setting in train the mathematical/philosophical gestation that would lead inexorably to the *Principia*. Despite himself Newton was drawn into a correspondence, which culminated in Hooke framing the problem exactly:

"It now remains to know the properties of a curve Line … made by a central attractive power … in a Duplicate proportion to the Distances reciprocally taken [in other words, obeying the inverse square rule]. I doubt not but that by your excellent method [Newton's calculus] you will easily find out what that Curve must be, and its properties, and suggest a physical Reason of this proportion."

Hooke had reached the limits of his abilities, and was forced to acknowledge that Newton had not. Yet the Cambridge man did not celebrate his triumph; he did not respond at all. Instead there was a long period of virtual silence, which would not be broken until a fateful visit four years later.

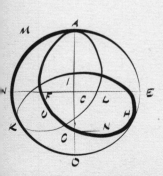

Newton went back and worked out the true path of descent: "An alternating ascent and descent"; in other words, an orbit.

Comets and Coffee Shops

FOR FOUR YEARS AFTER THE DISPUTE OVER THE SPIRAL TO THE CENTER OF THE EARTH, NEWTON GESTATED IDEAS OF FORCE AND MOTION, ATTRACTION AND ORBITS. COMETS CAME AND WENT, EACH ADDING A PIECE TO THE JIGSAW HE WAS PIECING TOGETHER IN HIS HEAD. FINALLY, IN 1684, A CONVERSATION IN A LONDON COFFEE HOUSE SENT A YOUNG ASTRONOMER ON A FATEFUL MISSION TO CAMBRIDGE.

Hooke's challenge to Newton had been to "find out what the Curve must be" for a body following an elliptical path around an attractor located at one focus (the point near one end of the ellipse around which the orbiting body swings). He went away and did just that, using his calculus to prove that for every point on the orbital path the curve followed the inverse square law. Previously he had considered the orbits of the planets as circular; now he was using mathematics to fit observations of the true, elliptical orbits of the planets to his 1666 insight about the inverse square law.

Coming into Focus

Later that year (1680) a comet appeared in the skies over Europe, and Newton entered into a correspondence with Astronomer Royal John Flamsteed about it (see pages 132–3), in which he clearly stated for the first time: "I can easily allow an attractive power in the Sun whereby the Planets are kept in their courses about him from going away in tangent lines." Two years later another comet (subsequently to become famous as Halley's Comet) appeared. Nature was playing its part in focusing Newton's mind on the problem of orbital mechanics.

Meanwhile, his researches on the nature of matter, begun through alchemy, were leading him to question one of the basic assumptions of natural philosophy, the existence of the ether. Newton had performed experiments that seemed to demon-

EDMOND HALLEY
From a wealthy family, youthful and handsome, sociable and adventurous, Halley was in many respects the polar opposite of Newton, yet he became one of the older man's greatest disciples. As a keen young astronomer fresh out of college he made his name with an intrepid mission to the South Atlantic island of St. Helena to make observations of the southern skies. Later he assisted Flamsteed, the Astronomer Royal, although the latter man disliked him on account of his rumored atheism.

"In 1684 Dr Halley came to visit him at Cambridge [and] asked him what he thought the curve would be that would be described by the planets supposing the force of attraction towards the Sun to be reciprocal to the square of their distance from it. Sir Isaac replied immediately that it would be an ellipsis. The doctor struck with joy & amazement and asked him how he knew it. Why said he, I have calculated it..."

— ABRAHAM DE MOIVRE'S ACCOUNT OF HALLEY'S VISIT TO CAMBRIDGE.

strate that there was no ether. If there was no ether, Descartes' theory of vortices as the agent of transmission of force throughout the cosmos was baseless. If this was so, how else could the force of attraction, of gravitation, the concept that was coming into focus in Newton's mind, be explained? Thus he was led to consider the alchemical notion of active principles, of gravity as a sort of natural spirit, a force that could act at a distance across vast expanses of vacuum. One by one the elements of a grand design were coalescing. All that was required in order for them to crystallize, whole and perfect, was a seed.

Encounter in a Coffee Shop

Celestial mechanics were in the air in the 1680s. Many of the foremost minds of the time were thinking about how to explain the orbit of the planets, and by 1684 several people had spotted the inverse square law. Three such men were Edmond Halley, a young astronomer; Sir Christopher Wren, astronomer and architect; and Robert Hooke. One Wednesday in January of 1684 the three of them were discussing the topic at a coffee house in London; could the force attracting the planets to the Sun, Halley wondered, decrease as an inverse square of the distance? Whereupon Hooke, Halley later wrote, "affirmed that upon that principle all the Laws of the celestial motions were to be demonstrated, and that he himself had done it."

Wren was skeptical, and "said that he would give Mr Hooke or me 2 months time to bring him a convincing demonstration thereof, and besides the honour, he of us that did it, should have from him a present of a book of 40 shillings." Two months and more passed without Hooke making good his boast, and by August Halley decided to go to Cambridge and ask Newton.

Sir Christopher Wren

Wren, architect, natural philosopher, and former president of the Royal Society, offered the wager that sent Halley to Cambridge.

Genesis of the *Principia*

HALLEY SUCCEEDED IN SETTING IN MOTION THE GEARS OF NEWTON'S GREAT INTELLECT. HE ACCOMPLISHED THIS WHERE OTHERS—MOST NOTABLY HOOKE—HAD FAILED BECAUSE HE ASKED THE RIGHT QUESTION. INSTEAD OF ASKING NEWTON TO SPECULATE, OR TO RESPOND TO SPECULATION, HE ASKED HIM TO CALCULATE, TO PROVE BY MATHEMATICS. ONCE NEWTON STARTED, HE FOUND HE COULD NOT STOP. HIS RESPONSE TO HALLEY GREW FROM A NINE-PAGE TREATISE TO AN ENTIRE BOOK.

Halley had gone to Cambridge in the hope that Newton could provide what Hooke apparently could not—mathematical proof that the motion of the planets was governed by the inverse square law, and that this could account for their elliptical orbits. His immediate reaction was joy, for Newton said that he had indeed calculated just such a proof. But frustration was to follow. According to French mathematician and Newton devotee Abraham De Moivre: "…Dr Halley asked him for his calculation … Sir Isaac looked among his papers but could not find it, but he promised him to renew it, & send it."

Set in Motion

Newton hated to send his handiwork out into the world without being very sure it was unimpeachably accurate, so it is entirely possible that he was lying to Halley and simply wanted the chance to check his calculations before handing them over. Whatever his initial intention, the project quickly mutated into something far grander.

At first Newton redid his calculations on the ellipse, supposedly by an entirely different mathematical route from before but with equally impressive results. These he wrote up in a nine-page treatise, "De Motu Corporum in Gyrum" ("On the Motion of Revolving Bodies"), which he had hand-delivered to Halley. Excited, the young astronomer rushed up to Cambridge to beg permission to show it to the Royal Society, and then hurried back to present it to a meeting on December 10, where the minutes recorded that "Mr Newton … had showed him a curious treatise." The "De Motu" manuscript created a tremendous buzz, John Flamsteed complaining that, "I believe I shall not get a sight of [it] till our common friend Mr Hooke & the rest of the town have first been satisfied."

A Search into Those Matters

Now that Halley's question had provided the seed, a vast and intricate design began to crystallize in Newton's mind, supersaturated as it was with the elements for a revolutionary new system of the world. One line of thought led him to another, and although Halley was pressing him for an immediate follow-up to "De Motu," he set his sights on something much grander:

"…after I had begun to consider the inequalities of the lunar motions, and had entered upon some other things relating to the laws and measures of gravity, and other forces; and the figures that would be described by bodies attracted according to given laws; and the motion of several bodies moving among themselves; the motion of bodies in resisting mediums; the forces, densities, and motions, of mediums; the

French mathematician Abraham De Moivre, to whom is owed an account of the genesis of the *Principia* and of Newton's earlier mathematical education.

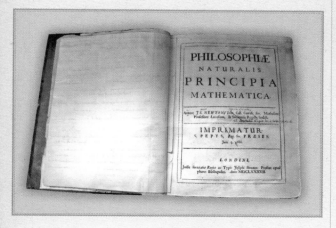

The frontispiece of Book I of the *Principia*, publication of which was overseen (and heavily subsidized) by Edmond Halley.

orbits of the comets, and such like; deferred that publication till I had made a search into those matters, and could put forth the whole together."

Another Archimedes

The new project engaged all Newton's prodigious mental energies. Humphrey Newton recalled the intensity of his labors at that time:

"Thinking all hours lost that were not spent in his studies, to which he kept so close that he seldom left his chamber ... So intent, so serious [was he] ... that he ate very sparingly, nay sometimes he forgot to eat at all ... When he sometimes took a turn or two [in the garden], he made a sudden stand, turned himself about, ran up the stairs like another Archimedes, with an 'eureka!' fell to write on his desk standing, without giving himself the leisure to draw a chair to sit down on."

The fruit of these labors was a growing manuscript, the first part of which was "put into the hands of Mr Halley" in April 1686. Its title: *Philosophiae Naturalis Principia Mathematica (Mathematical Principles of Natural Philosophy).*

"...it was to [Edmond Halley's] solicitations that [the *Principia*] becoming public is owing; for when he had obtained of me my demonstrations of the figure of the celestial orbits, he continually pressed me to communicate the same to the Royal Society, who afterwards, by their kind encouragement and entreaties, engaged me to think of publishing them."

— PREFACE TO THE FIRST EDITION OF *PRINCIPIA*

Laws of Motion

**NEWTON INTENDED THE
PRINCIPIA TO PRESENT A
PERFECT WHOLE, A SYSTEM
OF LAWS AND AXIOMS, EACH
PROVED BY MATHEMATICS
AND BUTTRESSED BY DEMON-
STRATIONS. IT WAS TO BE A
SYSTEM BUILT FROM THE
GROUND UP, USING BUILDING
BLOCKS OF NEWTON'S OWN
INVENTION. OFTEN THESE
BUILDING BLOCKS USED TERMS
AND CONCEPTS ALREADY IN
USE BUT HAZILY DEFINED,
SO HE BEGAN BY GIVING
PRECISE, FIXED DEFINITIONS,
AND USED THESE TO SPELL
OUT INFALLIBLE LAWS OF
FORCE AND MOTION.**

Much of Book I of the *Principia* was an expansion of "De Motu." It started with definitions of concepts such as mass and inertia, making precisely clear how they were related to but not the same as qualities such as volume, weight, and velocity. For instance, under the heading "Definition II" he wrote: "The quantity of motion is the measure of the same, arising from the velocity and quantity of matter conjunctly." Inertia was a concept he had adapted from Descartes, but he made it his own: "A body, from the inactivity of matter, is not without difficulty put out of its state of rest or motion. Upon which account [it] may, by a most significant name, be called vis inertiæ, or force of inactivity."

Time, Space, and Motion

He stated in the introduction his three famous laws of motion, but to give them meaning he first redefined time and space. These were words familiar from everyday use, but for Newton this meant they were unfit for purpose. To allow the sort of mathematical precision he required, he first had to establish them in their purest, original forms, rescuing them from the subjective experience of mere mortals:

"Absolute, true, and mathematical time, in and of itself, and of its own nature, without reference to anything external, flows uniformly…"

"Absolute space, of its own true nature without reference to anything external, always remains homogeneous and immovable…"

Centuries later, Einstein would prove a very different account of time and space, but he himself rejected claims that he had "destroyed" or "disproved" Newton's theory: "Let no one suppose that the mighty work of Newton can really be superseded by this or any other theory."

Newton was careful to distinguish absolute motion from relative motion, using the example of a ship under sail, and describing the relative and absolute motions of a sailor on the ship:

"As if that part of the earth, where the ship is, was truly moved toward the east, with a velocity of 10010 parts; while the ship itself, with fresh gale, and full sails, is carried towards the west, with a velocity expressed by 10 of those parts; but a sailor walks in the ship towards the east, with 1 part of the said velocity; then the sailor will be moved truly in immovable space towards the east, with a velocity of 10001 parts, and relatively on the earth towards the west, with a velocity of 9 of those parts."

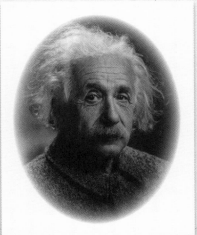

Albert Einstein (1879–1955) is often said to have made Newtonian physics obsolete; Einstein himself insisted he had done no such thing.

Raising a ball gives it potential energy.

Conservation is not perfect as energy is lost to sound, heat, and so on.

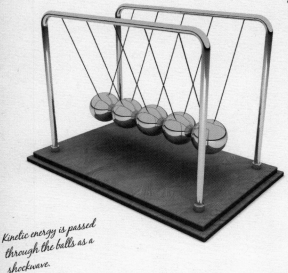

Newton's cradle, an executive toy created in the 20th century, which demonstrates the principle of conservation of momentum.

Kinetic energy is passed through the balls as a shockwave.

MATHEMATICAL PHILOSOPHY

Books I and II are mainly composed of geometrical proofs and demonstrations such as one would find in Euclid. Rather than using his calculus, Newton proved everything by the more laborious but traditional geometrical analysis. The first ten sections of the *Principia* contain almost no physics; although the subject is bodies in motion, the method is points, lines, and curves. Within the first few lines of his preface to the book, Newton defended his approach, citing the ancient and modern legitimacy of experiment and mathematics:

"Since the ancients ... made great account of the science of mechanics in the investigation of natural things; and the moderns, laying aside substantial forms and occult qualities, have endeavoured to subject the phænomena of nature to the laws of mathematics, I have in this treatise cultivated mathematics so far as it regards philosophy."

"Law 1: Every body perseveres in its state of being at rest or of moving uniformly straight forward, except insofar as it is compelled to change its state by force impressed.

Law 2: The change of momentum of a body is proportional to the impulse impressed on the body, and happens along the straight line on which that impulse is impressed.

Law 3: For a force there is always an equal and opposite reaction: or the forces of two bodies on each other are always equal and are directed in opposite directions."

— NEWTON'S LAWS OF MOTION

A System of the World

WHILE BOOKS I AND II SET OUT LAWS OF FORCES AND MOTION, BOOK III SHOWED THE APPLICATIONS OF THESE LAWS, INCLUDING THE THEORY OF UNIVERSAL GRAVITATION. IN LAYING OUT HIS THEORY OF AN ATTRACTIVE FORCE OPERATING BETWEEN ALL BODIES, OVER VAST DISTANCES OF INTERSTELLAR VACUUM, NEWTON DREW ON ALL HIS RESOURCES—MATHEMATICAL, ASTRONOMICAL, AND EVEN ALCHEMICAL. USING HIS THEORY HE THEN SET ABOUT EXPLAINING "THE MOTIONS OF THE PLANETS, THE COMETS, THE MOON, AND THE SEA," WITH A MATHEMATICAL PRECISION UNIQUE IN HISTORY.

Early in Book I Newton formalized the concept of gravity: "A centripetal force is that by which bodies are drawn or impelled, or any way tend, towards a point as a centre."

"Of this sort is gravity, by which bodies tend to the centre of the earth ... and that force, whatever it is, by which the planets are perpetually drawn aside from the rectilinear motions, which otherwise they would pursue, and made to revolve in curvilinear orbits."

Then he explained how the orbit of the Moon could be used to work out the force of gravity:

"If this force [gravity] was too small, it would not sufficiently turn the moon out of a rectilinear course: if it was too great, it would turn it too much, and draw down the moon from its orbit towards the earth. It is necessary, that the force be of a just quantity, and it belongs to the mathematicians to find the force, that may serve exactly to retain a body in a given orbit, with a given velocity..."

And eventually he stated the principle of universal gravitation: "at equal distances, it [the force of gravity] is the same everywhere; because (taking away, or allowing for the resistance of the air), it equally accelerates all falling bodies, whether heavy or light, great or small."

Knowledge is Power

Newton called the third book his "system of the world," explaining that:

"In the third book we give an example of this in the explication of the System of the World; for by the propositions mathematically demonstrated in the former books, we in the third derive from the celestial phænomena the forces of gravity with which bodies tend to the sun and the several planets. Then from these forces, by other propositions which are also mathematical, we deduce the motions of the planets, the comets, the moon, and the sea."

"...if it universally appears, by experiments and astronomical observations, that all bodies about the earth gravitate towards the earth ... that the moon likewise ... gravitates towards the earth; that ... our sea gravitates towards the moon; and all the planets mutually one towards another; and the comets in like manner towards the sun; we must ... universally allow that all bodies whatsoever are endowed with a principle of mutual gravitation."— NEWTON'S *PRINCIPIA*

Having set out his principles of mathematical philosophy, he demonstrated their power by using them to explain everything from the perturbations in the orbit of Saturn (due to "the action of Jupiter upon Saturn," which causes "a perturbation of the orb of Saturn in every conjunction of this planet with Jupiter, so sensible, that astronomers are puzzled with it") to the movement of the tides on Earth. He even calculated the density of air at great heights above the Earth and the force of gravity on other planets and worked out their masses and densities. For instance, he worked out that something that weighs 10,000 kg on the surface of the Sun will weigh 435 kg on the surface of the Earth. This is remarkably close to the figures that have been calculated using modern methods. He showed how the Earth is not a sphere but an oblate spheroid (egg-shaped), and how this shape interacts with the gravitational pull of the Sun and Moon to produce a wobble in the diurnal rotation that can account for the precession of the equinoxes (changes in the timing of the equinoxes over centuries), a mystery that had perplexed astronomers for millennia.

Galileo Galilei
1564–1642

Johannes Kepler
1571–1630

Marrying Galileo and Kepler

In the third book of the *Principia* Newton achieved the synthesis of the two major strands of natural philosophy. Galileo had explored earthly mechanics, with experiments on force and motion; and Kepler's laws had provided celestial mechanics. But no one had come close to marrying the two. This synthesis stands comparison with the greatest achievements of modern science, yet Newton accomplished it single-handedly in the space of two decades.

"A leaden ball, projected from the top of a mountain by the force of gunpowder … so that it might never fall to the Earth…"

UNFINISHED BUSINESS
Newton returned to the calculation that had stumped him during the plague years—comparing the force of gravity on Earth to the force keeping the Moon in its orbit. With a better estimate of the size of the Earth he was able to calculate that if the same force was at work, gravity at the surface of the Earth should cause a body to fall at just over 181 inches per second (460 cm/sec): "And heavy bodies do actually descend to the earth with this very force."

Rules for Philosophy

THE *PRINCIPIA* IS PRIMARILY FAMOUS FOR WHAT IT DISCOVERED ABOUT THE UNIVERSE (THE THEORY OF GRAVITY, THE LAWS OF MOTION, EXPLANATIONS OF PHYSICAL PHENOMENA), BUT SCIENTISTS ALSO CELEBRATE THE BOOK BECAUSE IT TELLS US HOW TO DISCOVER THINGS. PREVIOUSLY NATURAL PHILOSOPHERS HAD RELIED ON LOGIC, AUTHORITY, AND SOMETIMES EXPERIENCE, AND THE RESULTS WERE SPECULATION, HYPOTHESIS, AND OPINION. HOWEVER, IN THE *PRINCIPIA* NEWTON DEMONSTRATED A NEW WAY OF DOING PHILOSOPHY: THE SCIENTIFIC METHOD.

From the difficult reception of his theory of light and color Newton had learned that his approach was ahead of its time. Accordingly he devoted whole sections of the book to making it quite clear what his approach consisted of, and how it was different from anything that had gone before.

Spelling it Out

This approach had several important characteristics. It rejected a priori assumptions (assumptions about the way the world is which are based on untested received wisdom). For instance, Newton wrote that: "The common people conceive those quantities [time, space, place, and motion] under no other notions but from the relation they bear to sensible objects. And thence arise certain prejudices…"

He insisted on the legitimacy and necessity of experiment, a practice dismissed by traditional scholasticism as "mere mechanics": "the errors are not in the art, but in the artificers. He that works with less accuracy is an imperfect mechanic; and if any could work with perfect accuracy, he would be the most perfect mechanic of all; for the description of right lines and circles, upon which geometry is founded, belongs to mechanics…"

He spelled out how to build up a complete theory from first propositions, circumventing the fallibility of subjective experience: "Our design not respecting arts, but philosophy, and our subject not manual but natural powers … we offer this work as the mathematical principles of philosophy; for all the difficulty of philosophy seems to consist in this – from the phænomena of motions to investigate the forces of nature, and then from these forces to demonstrate the other phænomena…"

He was careful strictly to limit himself to what could be proved. Newton's system of the world was not simply opinion or speculation; it was fact, and he wanted to make that very clear: "In this philosophy particular propositions are inferred from the phænomena, and afterwards rendered general by induction. Thus it was that the

A sketch from William of Occam's 1341 manuscript of *Summa Logicae*.

"We are certainly not to relinquish the evidence of experiments for the sake of dreams and vain fictions of our own devising."

— NEWTON'S *PRINCIPIA*

impenetrability, the mobility, and the impulsive force of bodies, and the laws of motion and of gravitation, were discovered. And to us it is enough that gravity does really exist, and act according to the laws which we have explained, and abundantly serves to account for all the motions of the celestial bodies, and of our sea."

Against Dreams and Vain Fictions

Newton even included a special section of the book laying out rules for philosophy. Rule I, for instance, was a restatement of the famous principle known as Occam's Razor:

"We are to admit no more causes of natural things than such as are both true and sufficient to explain their appearances."

"To this purpose the philosophers say that Nature does nothing in vain, and more is in vain when less will serve; for Nature is pleased with simplicity, and affects not the pomp of superfluous causes."

In Rule IV he stated his allegiance to the inductive method, a form of reasoning championed by Sir Francis Bacon in which general laws are derived from analyzing specific instances (such as experimental evidence or astronomical observations), and set out one of the fundamental laws of the scientific method:

"In experimental philosophy we are to look upon propositions collected by general induction from phænomena as accurately or very nearly true, notwithstanding any contrary hypotheses that may be imagined, till such time as other phænomena occur, by which they may either be made more accurate, or liable to exceptions."

"This rule we must follow, that the argument of induction may not be evaded by hypotheses."

Just the Facts

But Newton was careful not to speculate beyond what he could prove. He had proved the existence of universal gravitation, but he was not going to speculate as to "the cause of this power," for as he wrote: "hitherto I have not been able to discover the cause of those properties of gravity from phænomena, and I frame no hypotheses ... wherefore, the reader is not to imagine, that ... I anywhere take upon me to define the kind, or the manner of any action, the causes or the physical reason thereof..."

The Scientific Method

Observation

↓

Question

↓

Hypothesis

↓

Experiment

↙   ↘

Accept
hypothesis

Reject
hypothesis

A flow chart laying out the basic process of the scientific method. Only once a hypothesis has been validated by experiment does it graduate to the status of a theory.

Little Smatterers

THE *PRINCIPIA* IS NOT AN EASY READ. ENTIRELY WRITTEN IN LATIN, IT IS COMPOSED MAINLY OF DIFFICULT GEOMETRY DEMONSTRATIONS. EVEN EXPERIENCED MATHEMATICIANS FOUND IT HARD GOING, AND ONE WAG AT CAMBRIDGE WAS FAMOUSLY MOVED TO OBSERVE ON CATCHING SIGHT OF PROFESSOR NEWTON: "THERE GOES THE MAN THAT WRIT A BOOK NEITHER HE NOR ANYBODY ELSE UNDERSTANDS." BUT WHY DID NEWTON MAKE HIS MASTERWORK SO HARD TO COMPREHEND?

In an unguarded moment Newton once revealed to a friend that the reason he had made the *Principia* so unreadable was "to avoid being bated by little smatterers in mathematics." With his almost hysterical fear of contradiction inflamed by sore memories of having to engage in debate over his theory of color with men he considered to be his intellectual inferiors, he had no intention of making the book accessible to anyone who could not appreciate the crushing force of his arguments—his proofs.

To Prevent Disputes

Indeed the introduction to Book III of the *Principia* suggests that he had initially considered a more accessible tome, but could not bear to be misunderstood:

"I now demonstrate the frame of the System of the World. Upon this subject I had, indeed, composed the third Book in a popular method, that it might be read by many; but afterward, considering that such as had not sufficiently entered into the principles could not easily discern the strength of the consequences, nor lay aside the prejudices to which they had been many years accustomed, therefore, to prevent the disputes which might be raised upon such accounts, I chose to reduce the substance of this Book into the form of Propositions (in the mathematical way), which should be read by those only who had first made themselves masters of the principles established in the preceding Books."

He warned the "common reader": "not that I would advise any one to the previous study of every Proposition of those Books; for they abound with such as might cost too much time, even to readers of good mathematical learning." Asked by a friend what books should be read in preparation for an attempt on the *Principia*, Newton airily detailed a daunting reading list:

"After Euclid's *Elements* [which consisted of 14 volumes], the elements of the conic sections are to be understood. And for this end you may read either the first part of the *Elementa Curvarum* of John de Witt, or de La Hire's late treatise of the conic sections or Dr Barrow's epitome of Apollonius. For algebra read first Bartholin's instruction & then peruse such problems as you will find scattered up & down in the *Commentaries on Carte's Geometry* & other algebraic writings of Francis Schooten... For astronomy read ... Gassendus's *Astronomy* & ... Mercator's *Astronomy*... These are sufficient..."

Euclid, whose *Elements* of *Geometry* Newton deemed required reading for those who wished to tackle the *Principia*.

"Philosophy is such an impertinently litigious Lady that a man had as good be engaged in Law suits as have to do with her."

GERARD — MERCATOR

Mr. Hooke's Pretensions

Book III of the *Principia* came near to being unwritten. Halley, as clerk of the Royal Society, had taken delivery of the first part of the manuscript and was shepherding its progress to publication. Parts of the work were read at a meeting of April 21, 1686, and Hooke was annoyed to hear that Newton failed to give proper credit to his own speculations on gravity, contained in the *System of the World* he had published 20 years earlier. Halley was forced to write to Newton: "Mr Hooke has some pretensions upon the invention of the rule of gravity... He says you had the notion from him..."

Predictably Newton was incandescent: "Now is this not very fine? Mathematicians that ... do all the business must content themselves with being nothing but dry calculators & drudges & another that does nothing but pretend & grasp at all things must carry away all the invention..." He raged on in this fashion, eventually concluding, "the third [book] I now design to suppress." In fact, this threat was never made good; Newton contented himself with systematically erasing every mention of Hooke's name from the entire *Principia*. The third part of the manuscript was delivered to Halley on April 4, 1687, and was published three months later.

Francis Willoughby, the ichthyologist whose 1678 magnum opus, *The History of Fishes*, was the first and nearly the last book published by the Royal Society, which was almost bankrupted by the cost of printing and could only publish the *Principia* with financial help from Halley.

THE ANCIENT WAY
Modern students using calculus can understand the propositions contained in the *Principia* with relative ease, but Newton was careful not to employ his new system of mathematical analysis in the book, for reasons he later made clear: "because the Ancients for making things certain admitted nothing into geometry before it was demonstrated synthetically, [I have ensured] that the System of the Heavens might be founded upon good Geometry. And this makes it now difficult for such unskilful men to see the Analysis by which those Propositions were found out."

Chapter Six

Love, Madness, and the Mint

A Time of Change

WRITING IN THE JOURNAL OF THE ROYAL SOCIETY, HALLEY GREETED THE AUTHOR OF THE *PRINCIPIA* WHO HAD "AT LENGTH BEEN PREVAILED UPON TO APPEAR IN PUBLICK." HAVING FINALLY TAKEN THE "PUBLICK" STAGE, NEWTON WOULD INCREASINGLY MOVE TOWARD ITS CENTER, BECOMING INVOLVED FOR THE FIRST TIME IN POLITICS, FORGING LINKS WITH THE MOST INFLUENTIAL MEN IN THE COUNTRY, AND EVEN TAKING ON THE KING.

The years following the publication of the *Principia* saw great changes overtake the life of Isaac Newton. From being an isolated, parochial figure, with horizons limited to a small portion of Lincolnshire and Cambridge, engaged in largely solitary and esoteric pursuits, he transformed into an international celebrity and political heavyweight, engaged in public life at the highest level. His circle of acquaintances would widen dramatically, bringing new intimacies and vulnerability to his life.

A Dispute with the King

While Newton had been engaged in writing the *Principia*, Britain had come to the brink of another civil war. Charles II had died in February 1685 (possibly as a result of dabbling in alchemy), and his brother had acceded to the throne as James II. The new king's Catholic sympathies promised to throw the nation into turmoil as he attempted to place Catholics in positions of power in major institutions, the universities included. James's efforts to force Catholic fellows and officers on the Cambridge colleges came to a head in the February of 1687, when the king ordered that a Benedictine monk, Father Alban Francis, be given a master's degree "without administering unto him any oath or oaths whatsoever" (in other words, with an exemption from the normal oaths to the Anglican Church). Newton, a virulent anti-Catholic, promptly waded into the row.

He began in typical fashion with voluminous research, digesting all the relevant documents—the university's charter, the Act of Incorporation, and various statutes and patents—and coming to the conclusion that the king was out of order: "Those that counselled his Majesty to disoblige the University cannot be his true friends... Be courageous therefore & steady to the Laws... If one P[apist] be a Master you may have a hundred... An honest Courage in these matters will secure all, having Law on our sides." He insisted that no one could be admitted to a degree "unless he take the Oaths," conveniently forgetting that this was exactly what he had done as a result of his Arianism.

Unlike his successor, Charles II had maintained a delicate balance between his Catholic sympathies and the anti-Catholic mood of the country.

"[The Marquis de L'Hôpital] cried out with admiration 'Good god what a fund of knowledge there is in that book'. He then asked ... every particular about Sir I, even to the colour of his hair, and said: does he eat & drink & sleep? Is he like other men?"

The House of Commons, where Newton served as a Member of Parliament, though supposedly his only contribution was to complain of a draft.

Fortunately for Newton nobody spotted his blatant hypocrisy, even when he entered the fray directly, becoming one of the vice-chancellor's advisors and being appointed as a representative to the commission that the king had convened to impose his will on the university. Although the Cambridge delegation was unsuccessful in its bid to oppose the king, events would soon render the issue moot. A year later James had been deposed and the throne was back in Protestant hands. The Dutch Prince William of Orange and his English wife were placed on the throne in the Glorious Revolution of 1688. The new order brought opportunity for men such as Newton.

Friends in High Places

The Father Francis episode had a profound impact on Newton; he had tasted authority and he liked it. The new king called a new Parliament, and the university turned to Newton as its candidate. By January 1689 Newton was sitting as a Member of Parliament and dining with the king. An extended stay in London offered the opportunity to make influential new friends, including Charles Mordaunt, the Earl of Monmouth; Charles Montagu, a rising star of English politics; and John Locke, the philosopher (and fellow secret alchemist), who described his new friend as "the incomparable Mr Newton" in the preface to his 1690 masterpiece *An Essay Concerning Human Understanding*.

All the while Newton's renown was spreading within intellectual circles, as copies of the *Principia* filtered into Europe and philosophers began to grasp the magnitude of his achievement. The new hero of natural philosophy was beginning to attract hero-worshipers.

NEWTON THE TIPSTER
The president of the Royal Society at the time of the publication of the *Principia* was Samuel Pepys, the diarist. He had little understanding of science, but a keen appreciation of its applications; in 1693 he approached Newton for help with calculating probabilities in a dice game on which he was fond of wagering money. Newton obliged, explaining why it was better to wager money on the likelihood of throwing a single six with six dice than double sixes with twelve dice.

Newton's Ape

AMONG THOSE DRAWN INTO NEWTON'S ORBIT WAS A YOUNG SWISS MATHEMATICIAN NAMED NICHOLAS FATIO DE DUILLIER, OR FATIO FOR SHORT. FATIO QUICKLY SET HIMSELF UP AS NEWTON'S PRODIGY AND CHEERLEADER, CLAIMING TO BE THE EDITOR OF A PLANNED SECOND EDITION OF THE *PRINCIPIA*, BUT AROUND LONDON HE WAS DISPARAGINGLY KNOWN AS THE "APE OF NEWTON." BUT WHAT WAS THE TRUE NATURE OF THE RELATIONSHIP BETWEEN THE TWO MEN?

Already Newton was planning for a second edition of the *Principia*. He hoped to make an exact description of the lunar orbit its centerpiece, and started to pursue the data he needed, also wrestling with some of the profound issues he had left out of the first edition. What was gravity? What was its mechanism? Could he construct a unified theory that would explain subatomic forces such as those that governed chemical reactions and magnetism, and link them with gravity and mechanics?

Nicholas Fatio de Duillier
1664–1753

The Way to Chastity

All the while Newton struggled with less elevated thoughts, admitting that, through too much thinking, "the body is also put out of its due temper & for want of sleep the fansy is invigorated about what ever it sets it self upon & by degrees inclines towards a delirium in so much that those Monks who fasted most arrived to a state of seeing apparitions of women & their shapes..." But it was not women whose shapes he saw.

Nicholas Fatio de Duillier was from a wealthy Swiss family. Expensively educated and with a talent for self-promotion, he gained a reputation as a prodigy. In 1687, aged 23, he was described as "one of the greatest men of his age, who seems born to carry learning some sizes beyond what it has attained."

In June of that year, having won the favor of William of Orange by warning him of a plot against his life, he came to London armed with glowing letters of introduction, and immediately got himself elected as a fellow of the Royal Society. Two years later he was accorded the honor of escorting the great Dutch philosopher Christiaan Huygens to London, presenting him to a meeting of the Society on June 12, where he first met Newton.

"I ... last night received your letter with which how much I was affected I cannot express..." — FROM A LETTER FROM NEWTON TO FATIO

Love Letters

The two quickly became as thick as thieves, meeting frequently, discussing philosophy, alchemy, and religion and carrying on a lively correspondence, surviving examples of which hint at something more than friendship, not least because they were censored by officious hands. "I intend to be in London the next week & should be very glad to be in the same lodging with you. I will bring my books and your letters with me," wrote Newton, following it up a few weeks later with: "Pray let me know by a line or two whether you can have lodgings for both of us in the same house at present or whether you would have me take some other lodgings for a time 'til [censored]."

Fatio appointed himself Newton's number one disciple, spreading the good word about his master's works in letters to Continental Europe in which he sung Newton's praises—"The most honest man I know and the ablest mathematician who has ever lived"—and declared that Cartesianism was now shown to be nothing but "an empty imagination."

Over the next four years Newton would allow the younger man into his confidence to an extraordinary degree. Not only did Fatio begin to boast that he would take charge of the second edition of the *Principia* (which he intended to expand greatly with additions of his own), but Newton shared with him secret alchemical and religious researches, even to the extent of revealing his closely guarded Arianism. This was surely the most intimate relationship of his adult life.

A VOLUNTARY AGENT

What was the role of God in Newton's vision of the cosmos? "Can God be nowhere when the moment of time is everywhere?" he pondered in an unpublished draft piece. It is commonplace nowadays to ascribe the ascent of the atheistic materialist worldview to the success of Newton's system of the world, but he himself would never have countenanced such a view, writing that he did not think the organization of the cosmos "explicable by mere natural causes but am forced to ascribe it to the counsel & contrivance of a voluntary Agent."

God imbues Adam with life. Newton was profoundly religious, viewing his philosophical investigations as a kind of sacrament.

Break-Up

NEWTON SEEMS TO HAVE BEEN IN THE GRIP OF A POWERFUL INFATUATION. WAS FATIO DE DUILLIER A WORTHY OBJECT FOR THIS OBSESSION? THEIR CORRESPONDENCE TOOK ON THE NATURE OF A COURTSHIP: IMPLORING LETTERS WERE MET WITH TEASING PROMISES, PLANS WITH PREVARICATION, ARDENT DESIRE WITH DISMAY. HAVING MADE HIMSELF VULNERABLE NEWTON NOW PAID THE PRICE, AND IT VERY NEARLY COST HIM HIS SANITY.

By the beginning of 1690 their relationship was such that Fatio could tease his mentor (about his poor French) in a manner unthinkable from anyone else. Expecting a copy of Huygens's new book *Traité de la Lumière* (*Treatise on Light*), the young Swiss cheekily suggested that, "It being written in French, you may perhaps choose rather to read it here with me." In June of that year Fatio embarked on a 15-month tour of Europe; Newton's distress at this separation can be guessed at from an uncharacteristically anxious note to Locke, inquiring whether there had been any word of the young mathematician. When Fatio got back in September 1691 Newton rushed down to London to greet him at the docks; significantly, this trip was kept secret from even his closest friends and Newton neglected to sign out of the college register.

"My Head Is Out of Order"

In November Fatio visited Cambridge, but fell ill on his return to London, penning a plaintive missive to Newton on November 17, 1692: "With coming from Cambridge I got a grievous cold, which is fallen upon my lungs... I thank God my soul is extremely quiet, in which you have had the chief hand. My head is something out of order, and I suspect will grow worse and worse... If I am to depart this life I could wish my eldest brother ... could succeed me in Your friendship." These sentiments were accompanied by a detailed account of his aches and pains. Newton was badly scared—"I ... last night received your letter with which how much I was affected I cannot express..." —but, in fact, by the time his letter had reached Newton, Fatio had recovered (he would live to a ripe old age).

Fatio's ill health (or hypochondria) rumbled on and in January 1693 Newton wrote with a proposal: "I fear the London air conduces to your indisposition & therefore wish you would remove hither so soon as the weather will give you leave to take a journey." But he did not receive the response he was hoping for: Fatio was considering moving back to Switzerland.

More letters passed between them, and the young Swiss seemed either to be teasing the older man or demanding a dangerously indiscreet declaration: "if you wish I should go there [to Cambridge] ... for some other reasons than what barely relates to my health and to the saving of charges [expenses] I am ready to do so; but I could wish in that case you would be plain in your next letter." Still more revealing was a letter he sent to his older brother in Switzerland: "My pain comes chiefly from a cause that I cannot explain here ... the reasons I should not marry will probably last as long as my life."

Newton and Fatio exchanged a flurry of letters, but when the correspondence was broken off the older man was plunged into despair.

The Tower of London

A late-17th-century print of the Tower of London from *A Book of the Prospects of the Remarkable Places in and about the City of London.*

"If It Was Possible"

Yet still he did not come to Cambridge. In March Newton wrote that, "The chamber next to me is disposed of [available]…" and offered, "to make you such an allowance as might make your subsistence here easy to you." Fatio waited a month to reply, and although he claimed "I could wish sir to live all my life … with you, if it was possible," it appears that it was not possible, for nothing came of Newton's many appeals.

He traveled down to London twice in late May and early June. No record of these meetings survives, but the once fervent correspondence between the two was abruptly broken off, plunging Newton into despair, even to the edge of madness. The conclusion seems inevitable: the relationship between the two men was more than platonic. Whether or not it was consummated, it seems clear that Newton was infatuated with the young Swiss, and that the breakdown of this intense relationship was more than his fragile psyche could bear.

"My pain comes chiefly from a cause that I cannot explain here … the reasons I should not marry will probably last as long as my life."

— Fatio de Duillier writing to his brother, 1692

Breakdown: A Black Year

THE TRIUMPH OF *PRINCIPIA* AND HIS SUDDEN ELEVATION TO CELEBRITY STATUS UNDER THE NEW REGIME LAUNCHED NEWTON INTO SEVERAL YEARS OF EUPHORIA, ENHANCED BY THE INTENSITY OF HIS EXCITING NEW RELATIONSHIP. IN 1693 EUPHORIA TURNED TO DESPAIR, AND NEWTON WAS PLUNGED DEEP INTO A "BLACK YEAR." RUMORS OF HIS DERANGEMENT SPREAD ACROSS EUROPE AND IT WAS SAID THAT HE WAS LOST TO PHILOSOPHY.

In May 1694 the Dutch natural philosopher Christiaan Huygens heard from a Scotsman named Colm that Isaac Newton had succumbed to an attack of frenzy that had lasted for 18 months, driven insane by incessant work and by the loss of many of his papers to a fire that had swept through his study. His friends had had him confined, the derangement of his senses confirmed by his inability to recognize his own masterwork, the *Principia*. Newton, Huygens sadly concluded, was lost to natural philosophy.

Legends of the Fall

Huygens passed on the story to the German mathematician and philosopher Leibniz, and it was soon circulating throughout Europe's intellectual community. In 1695 the rumor reached the ears of the philosopher-publisher John Wallis, who was visiting Germany. The fire had destroyed Newton's house and all his books, he was told by one Johann Sturm, and he was "so disturbed in mind thereupon, as to be reduced to very ill circumstances." Wallis denied the report, and indeed by this time Newton was his old self, feuding with rivals and pursuing the second edition of his *Principia*. Yet something strange had occurred—a severe crisis and a very real derangement.

Poison-Pen letters

For four months after his abrupt break with Fatio, Newton had retreated into isolation, plunging himself with renewed fervor into his alchemical studies. His friends heard nothing from him until, in mid-September 1693, two extraordinary letters were delivered to his friends Samuel Pepys and John Locke. On September 13 he wrote to Pepys (left).

Sir, -- Sometime after Mr. Millington had delivered your message he pressed me to see you the next time I went to London. I was averse, but, upon his pressing, consented, before I considered what I did; for I am extremely troubled at the embroilment I am in, and have neither ate nor slept well this twelvemonth, nor have my former consistency of mind. I never designed to get anything by your interest, nor by King James's favour; but am now sensible that I must withdraw from your acquaintance, and see neither you nor the rest of my friends any more, if I may but leave them quietly. I beg your pardon for saying I would see you again; and rest

Your most humble and obedient servant,

Is. Newton.

Three days later, from an inn in London, he sent Locke a bewildering apology (right).

Fortunately for Newton he had chosen two of the most sensitive and kindly men in England to startle in this fashion. Locke waited two weeks and then wrote a touching letter assuring Newton of his friendship. Pepys, who had sent no message by Mr. Millington, recruited his nephew in Cambridge to check up on the professor, who it seemed was now quite well. What had occasioned this extraordinary meltdown?

"I am extremely troubled at the embroilment I am in, and have neither ate nor slept well this twelvemonth, nor have my former consistency of mind."

Sir, -- Being of opinion that you endeavoured to embroil me with women, and by other means, I was so much affected with it as that when one told me that you were sickly and would not live, I answered "'twere better if you were dead." I desire you to forgive this uncharitableness, for I am now satisfied that what you have done is just, and I beg your pardon for my having hard thoughts of you for it; and for representing that you struck at the root of morality, in a principle you laid in your book of ideas, and designed to pursue in another book, and that I took you for a Hobbist. I beg your pardon also for saying or thinking that there was a design to sell me an office, or to embroil me.

I am your most humble and unfortunate servant,

Is. Newton.

LOCKE AND NEWTON
In the philosophical and political spheres, the philosopher John Locke can be considered the counterpart of Newton. He championed the philosophy of empiricism, arguing that knowledge is not innate but derives from experience; in Newton's commitment to the scientific method he saw this exemplified, and when they were introduced in 1689 it was a meeting of minds that shaped both their futures.

John Locke
1632–1704

The Philosopher's Bane

NEWTON'S SUDDEN DESCENT INTO MADNESS HAS PROVED FERTILE GROUND FOR HISTORICAL SPECULATION AND DETECTIVE WORK. BY HIS OWN ACCOUNT HE HAD NOT SLEPT FOR DAYS WHEN HE WROTE HIS STRANGE LETTERS, AND HIS BREAKDOWN CAME IN THE CONTEXT OF EMOTIONAL AND PROFESSIONAL STRESS. BUT COULD THERE HAVE BEEN AN EXTERNAL AGENT OF MADNESS AT WORK? MERCURY POISONING WAS AN OCCUPATIONAL HAZARD OF ALCHEMY; SYMPTOMS INCLUDE DERANGEMENT OF THE SENSES.

Newton was quick to apologize for his unaccountable lapses. He told Pepys's nephew Millington that he had written the "very odd letter … in a distemper that much seized his head, and that kept him awake for above five nights…" He elaborated a similar tale to Locke:

"The last winter by sleeping too often by my fire I got an ill habit of sleeping & a distemper which this summer has been epidemical put me further out of order, so that when I wrote to you I had not slept an hour a night for a fortnight together & for 5 nights together not a wink. I remember I wrote to you but what I said of your book I remember not."

All this was now past, although Millington did add, "I fear he is under some small degree of melancholy…"

Mercury Madness

Newton's own diagnosis, "distemper," explains little: it means a derangement of the humors, which simply begs the question. More recent times have seen a number of explanations surface, the most popular of which is probably mercury poisoning. Mercury can be highly toxic, depending on the type of exposure; as a liquid it is relatively safe and has even been drunk and caused little harm. As a vapor, however, it can be absorbed through the lungs and cause long-lasting neurological problems, including confusion, memory loss, and paranoia, together with insomnia, all symptoms exhibited by Newton. Alchemical experiments often revolved around mercury, with constant heating that could easily produce clouds of vapor, and Newton's endeavors were no different. He was certainly at high risk of mercury poisoning, and it is suggestive that a period of renewed alchemical activity preceded his apparent derangement.

Analysis of surviving hair samples attributed to Newton would seem to lend some support to the theory, showing high levels of mercury. Given his lengthy pursuit of alchemy it would perhaps be surprising to find otherwise, but these analyses are far from conclusive. Apart from the problem of proving that the hair samples are genuine, it is not possible to pinpoint the mercury contamination. Importantly, Newton lacked many of

Mercury, or quicksilver. Once absorbed into the bloodstream, it can disrupt the metabolism of nerve cells and cause neurological problems.

"… when I wrote to you I had not slept an hour a night for a fortnight together & for 5 nights together not a wink." — FROM A LETTER FROM NEWTON TO LOCKE

To Kill a King

A much more plausible example than Newton of mercury poisoning was Charles II, who suddenly took ill in January 1685 with symptoms including convulsions and slurred speech. The king enjoyed dabbling in alchemy and had a laboratory in the basement of his palace at Westminster where he would attempt to "fix" mercury, a process that involved heating it. Analysis of surviving hair samples appears to show toxic levels of mercury, while an autopsy reported that his cerebrospinal fluid was cloudy, indicating damage to the blood–brain barrier consistent with massive acute mercury poisoning by vapor inhalation.

The Dead Alchemist, by Elihu Vedder. Inhalation of toxic fumes was an occupational hazard for alchemists. Mercury was particularly dangerous because its fumes were invisible and odorless.

the other telltale persistent symptoms of mercury poisoning: hand tremors, loss of teeth (at death he still possessed all but one of his teeth). Some authorities have claimed that his writing at this point becomes spidery, but Westfall disagrees: "Though I have been very attentive to Newton's hand, I am unable to discern such."

In fact, Newton's rapid recovery and his subsequent good health and longevity all count against chronic mercury poisoning as an explanation, but perhaps an acute episode occasioned by a single exposure to a toxic cloud of mercury vapor could still fit the facts.

A Fragile Psyche

It may not be necessary to invoke mercury, however. The evidence of Newton's early years and his ongoing feuds suggests that his psyche was fragile at best. In the context of several years of wholesale changes to his way of life and self-image, and particularly the emotional fallout of his relationship with Fatio and its abrupt termination, a psychological cause is not so hard to envisage. Locked away with his thoughts, confronted with feelings and desires he could barely comprehend let alone accept, deranged from lack of sleep: perhaps a nervous breakdown was inevitable.

The Mint

RESTORED TO HIS SENSES, NEWTON WAS NOW READY FOR A NEW CHALLENGE. ALTHOUGH IT SEEMED A LONG WAY FROM THE GLORIES OF HIS AMAZING SCIENTIFIC BREAKTHROUGHS, HIS NEXT ROLE WAS HUGELY IMPORTANT IN ITS OWN WAY, FOR HE WAS ABOUT TO BE HANDED RESPONSIBILITY FOR NOTHING LESS THAN SAVING THE COUNTRY FROM RUIN. APPOINTED WARDEN AT THE ROYAL MINT, NEWTON SOON PUT HIS OWN STAMP ON THE ANCIENT INSTITUTION.

One of the sources of Newton's depression may have been the tacit realization that, now into his 50s, his greatest intellectual accomplishments were behind him. He had not succeeded in discovering the unified theory he sought and was growing increasingly frustrated in his attempt to develop a comprehensive lunar theory. Newton needed a new challenge, one far from the arid time-servers of Cambridge academia, and he craved recognition and reward from the new regime.

Proof of Friendship

Attempts had been made since the Glorious Revolution to find a suitably rewarding civil post for Newton, but he was aligned with the Whig faction in British politics and the rival Tories held power at first. By 1695, however, things had changed. The Whigs swept into power and Newton's friend Montagu, whom he had known since undergraduate days, had been appointed chancellor of the exchequer. Rumors began to circulate that Newton was to be afforded a position at the Royal Mint, traditionally a lucrative sinecure—a job that required little or no effort, but which entitled the holder to a royalty on every coin minted.

Newton insisted it was untrue, writing to Halley on March 14, 1696 that, "if the rumour of preferment for me in the Mint should ... be revived, I pray that you would endeavour to obviate it..." Was he being disingenuous? Possibly so, since five days later a letter (see below) arrived from Montagu with news that cannot have come completely out of the blue: Newton was to be made the warden of the Mint.

Although subordinate to the master, the warden was notionally the chief operating officer at the Mint; traditionally the incumbents of both posts left any real work to subordinates,

Sir

I am very glad that at last I can give you good proof of my friendship ... the King has promised me to make Mr Newton Warden of the Mint, the office is the most proper for you it is the chief officer in the Mint, it is worth five or six hundred pounds per annum, and has not too much business to require more attendance than you can spare.

A Brief History of the Mint
King Edgar centralized English coinage in the ninth century: "Let one money pass throughout the king's dominion... Let one measure and one weight be used, such as is observed in London." By the end of the 13th century the Mint had moved to the Tower of London, around the same time as the post of master was created by Edward I.

Crest of the Royal Mint

"I swear that I will not reveal or discover to any person or persons whatsoever the new invention of rounding the money & making the edges of them with letters or graining or either of them directly or indirectly, so help me God."

— Oath sworn by Newton on his first morning at the Mint

hence, "not too much business to require more attendance than you can spare." Isaac Newton, however, did things differently.

Farewell Cambridge

On April 20, 1696, just four weeks after receiving the letter from Montagu, Newton left Trinity for the last time. He had long before given up the teaching aspects of his professorship; within five years he would give up the chair altogether. After 35 years at Cambridge he might be expected to have formed some attachments to places or people, yet he returned on just one occasion, for only a few days, and as far as is known never wrote a single letter to anybody at the university.

Charles Montagu (1661–1715), a poet who became a statesman and was later elevated to the peerage as the Earl of Halifax.

Arriving at the Tower, Newton would have found his quarters less than salubrious; the rooms were small, the garden received no sunlight, the noise from the stamps and presses was incessant from 4 o'clock in the morning to midnight, and the smell from 300 workers and dozens of horses considerable. A greater contrast with the quiet quadrangles of Trinity is hard to imagine, but Newton was unfazed. He was there to work, and he had arrived just in the nick of time to avert the nation's ruin.

Newton to the Rescue

NEWTON'S APPOINTMENT TO THE MINT CAME AT A TIME OF CRISIS FOR THE COUNTRY'S MONETARY SYSTEM. THE NATION'S COINAGE HAD BECOME DEBASED AND UNTRUSTWORTHY, AND THE ECONOMY WAS ON THE VERGE OF COLLAPSE. RECTIFYING THE PROBLEM WAS A MASSIVE UNDERTAKING REQUIRING ALL OF NEWTON'S ENERGY, RELENTLESS INTENSITY OF FOCUS, DILIGENCE, AND TECHNICAL SKILL. BUT IF HE WAS TO DO THE JOB, HE INSISTED ON DOING IT HIS WAY, AND AS USUAL WOULD BROOK NO DISSENT.

The problem of the national coinage had been worsening for decades, if not centuries. It was absolutely vital for the flow of commerce and the functioning of the economy that everyone could trust that a coin was worth what it claimed to be worth—in other words that it contained the specified weight of precious gold or silver. But years of inefficient operation had left the nation's money supply antiquated and prey to counterfeiters and clippers.

Bad Money

Many of the coins in circulation were Elizabethan, and some dated back as far as Edward VI. Crude minting techniques produced coins that were easy to counterfeit (with fakes made up of less precious metals like tin) and clip, where the edges of the coin were clipped off—the clippings would be gathered together, melted down, and cast into new coins or bullion, while the clipped coin was filed down and reshaped to appear legal. The scale of the problem was vast; when the old money supply was finally recalled, the weight of the coins taken in by the authorities was just 54 per cent of their legal weight. Shopkeepers could not trust their customers and raised prices to compensate. Wage earners could not trust the coin with which they were paid. Riots had become increasingly common.

The Recoinage

The introduction of milling technology from France in the 1660s had been intended to prevent clipping by supplying coins with milled and engraved edges that could not be replicated, but their introduction was bungled. Unscrupulous moneyers simply hoarded the valuable new coins and melted them down into bullion, which they could sell on at a profit. Newton's sponsor Montagu had initiated an ambitious recoinage project, in which old currency would be recalled en masse and huge numbers of milled coins would be minted to replace it. However, only an administrator of special gifts could hope to pull off such a complex program.

England's coinage was antique, with wear, damage, and mutilation diminishing its worth and undermining public confidence in the value of money.

The State of the Mint

Newton got to work as soon as he arrived. He was there to see in the first shift at 4 o'clock in the morning and the last shift at night.

Analyzing every step in the minting process, Newton identified inefficiencies and bottlenecks, streamlining and optimizing the operation. He put his alchemical expertise with metals to good use, ensuring that the raw materials were sourced at the

The Mint's milling or edging machine, which marked the edges of coins to prevent them from being clipped.

"Two mills with 4 millers, 12 horses, two horse keepers, 3 cutters, 2 flatters, 8 sizers, one nealer, three blanchers, two markers, two presses with fourteen labourers to pull at them can coin after the rate of a thousand weight or 3000 pounds of money per diem."

— NEWTON'S ANALYSIS OF THE MINTING PROCESS

best prices, and overseeing the technical details of smelting and minting. Under his expert guidance and relentless scrutiny, the Mint was transformed into a highly efficient organization. In the first four months of 1696 only around a third of a million pounds-worth of old coins had been swapped for new ones; by June 24, £4,706,003 had been reclaimed.

To achieve all this Newton needed two things: information and power. He approached the task as he always did: copious research led to systematic notes, under headings such as "Observations concerning the Mint," "Of the Assays," "Of the Making the Moneys." He became an expert on economics, currency systems, and financial theory. But the Mint was an ancient institution, hamstrung by petty fiefdoms and competing priorities; Newton became intent on expanding his authority, or, as he saw it, on reasserting the ancient prerogatives of the warden. In typical fashion he buried himself in historical documents and issued complex edicts summarizing his research. Echoes of his quest to discover the *prisca sapientia* and reconstitute the original, pure religion can clearly be heard in his 1696 report, "The State of the Mint": "the Warden's authority ... being baffled & rejected & thereby the government of the Mint being in a manner dissolved... Nor do I see any remedy more proper & more easy than by restoring the ancient constitution." By the time the incumbent master died in December 1699 and Newton succeeded him, he had already acquired more or less total control.

THE MILLER'S TALE
The key weapon in the battle against counterfeit and debased coin was the edging or milling machine. This had been invented in France, and anyone who could read French could find a description of such a machine easily enough, but the Mint took the security of the device very seriously, and Peter Blondeau, the man who had designed the machinery, personally edged every coin.

A Crusade of Vengeance

ONE BIZARRE ASPECT OF NEWTON'S INVOLVEMENT WITH THE MINT WAS THE MANNER IN WHICH HE PROSECUTED THE CRUSADE AGAINST COUNTERFEITERS AND OTHER CURRENCY CRIMINALS. HE NOT ONLY TOOK CHARGE OF THE PROCESS BUT ALSO BECAME PERSONALLY INVOLVED IN RUNNING A NETWORK OF INFORMANTS, HUNTING DOWN SUSPECTS, AND INTERROGATING PRISONERS; NEWTON WAS MERCILESS IN BRINGING THE FULL FORCE OF THE LAW TO BEAR.

Ever since childhood Newton had possessed an unpleasant side to his character, an implacable vengefulness and urge to dominate that spoke of deep-seated anger, possibly even psychotic tendencies. Now he found that he had the power of life and death, and he was remorseless in exercising it. Part of the warden's remit was to oversee the detection and capture of counterfeiters; normally they did not perform this function, but as the primary effort of recoinage relaxed in 1698, Newton embraced it.

Underworld

Newton set up a network of informers and agents in 11 counties, sometimes even paying them out of his own pocket; "paid £5 to Humphrey Hall to buy him a suit of clothes to qualify him for conversing with a gang of coiners of note," his minutely detailed notes recorded. His task was complicated by a well-meaning new law rewarding informers, which prompted a flurry of suspect allegations. Newton complained: "my agents & witnesses are discouraged and tired out by want of success & by the reproach of prosecuting and swearing for money."

He preferred to cultivate his own sources directly, and frequented the lowest dives in London in order to meet up with informers and follow leads. His expenses for this period include money spent at "taverns, prisons and other places in the prosecution of clippers and coiners." He paid to have himself made a justice of the peace in various counties so that he could stay in touch with the comings and goings of criminals. When suspects were brought in, Newton took personal charge of their interrogation. The records show that between June 1698 and December 1699 he cross-examined 200 suspects, informers, and witnesses.

"Criminals, like dogs, always return to their vomit."

— NEWTON PARAPHRASING PROVERBS 26:11

Newton vs. Chaloner

Newton became the scourge of the counterfeiting underworld. In one week in February 1699 he had ten prisoners in Newgate Prison awaiting hanging. He was merciless, not hesitating to have poor single mothers and their children intimately searched for a few stolen pennies, and implacable, as demonstrated by his run-in with notorious forger William Chaloner.

A bold and charismatic rogue with a public profile and taste for the high life, Chaloner had been in and out of prison. Newton succeeded in having him taken up to Newgate in 1697, but was thwarted when Chaloner's patrons in Parliament helped secure his acquittal. The warden would not give up easily, however, biding his time until January 1699 when an informer gave him the evidence he needed to have Chaloner locked up once more. This time Newton made no mistake; after several months of fruitless efforts to secure release, his prey made a final pathetic plea: "Save me from being murdered Oh! Dear Sir do this merciful deed." It fell on deaf ears, and on March 22 Chaloner was taken to Tyburn to be hanged, drawn, and quartered.

Such zeal made enemies. A surgeon at Newgate reported overhearing a conversation between prisoners: "Whitfield … made answer that the Warden of the Mint was a rogue and if ever King James came again he would shoot him, and then Ball made answer: God damn my blood so will I, and though I don't know him yet I'll find him out."

Gottfried Leibniz
1646–1716

Johann Bernoulli
1637–1748

BERNOULLI'S BRACHISTOCHRONE
In spite of his duties Newton still found time to exercise his mathematical prowess. In 1697 Swiss mathematician Johann Bernoulli, in league with Leibniz, cooked up an apparently insoluble problem—a *brachistochrone*—with which they hoped to embarrass Newton. In the thick of the frantic recoinage program, the Englishman managed to knock out a solution in a few hours, publishing it anonymously, although Bernoulli famously commented that he recognized the hand of Newton, "tanquam ex ungue leonem" ("as the lion is known by its claw").

The Society Restored

In 1701 Newton finally resigned the Lucasian Chair, severing his last link with Cambridge. Now he was a London man, subject to the tides of politics; the accession of Queen Anne to the throne in 1702 saw the removal of the Whigs from office, cutting Newton's power base from under him. Fortunately, however, a new opportunity arose with the death of his old nemesis Robert Hooke and the chance to take the helm of another great institution, the Royal Society.

By the start of the 18th century the Royal Society was sadly diminished. From a high point of 200 in the 1670s the membership had nearly halved. Its finances were badly disordered and it was nearly bankrupt. Hanging over it was the threat of eviction from its habitual meeting rooms and library in Gresham College, which was being redeveloped.

A Very Proper Discourse?

The intellectual standing of the Society had also diminished as discussions became increasingly fatuous and rambling. The influence of prominent physicians such as Hans Sloane and John Woodward skewed coverage toward pseudo-medical chatter. For instance, in May 1699, Mr. Van de Bembde's remark that "cow's piss drank to about a pint, will either purge or vomit with great Ease" led to animated discussion of the therapeutic benefits of bovine urine. A typical discussion a month later saw Dr. Woodward offering the dubious insight that "it is not water that Nourishes but Earth," to which the vice president inexplicably replied "the best time to smell at flowers is in the Morning"; Dr. Sloane opined that this "was a very proper discourse for this place."

Taking the Reign

Despite being in London for several years now, Newton had scarcely attended a single meeting, undoubtedly due to the presence of his mortal enemy Robert Hooke. In March 1703, however, Hooke passed away, and at the next annual meeting on November 30 Newton was elected president. His psychoanalytic biographer, Frank Manuel, has made the point that whenever Newton identified himself with an institution, it became an extension of his personality. The Royal Society was to be no different. Newton set about taking complete control, transforming the fortunes of the Society with his usual energy and application.

He attended almost every meeting, missing just three in the first 20 years of his presidency, and commented on nearly every paper that was read. He was determined that the Royal

"The President was not prepared ... to enter upon the debate but freely (though methinks not very civilly) replied that he had good reasons for their removing which he did not think proper to be given there."

Society should fulfil what he saw as its original remit. He promptly named one new curator of experiments, and later a second—both his own men—and he encouraged the replication of experiments described in the papers.

Transformation was not achieved overnight, and the Royal Society was still partial to exhibits that were better fitted for the sideshow than the laboratory, such as "four Piggs all Growing to One Another taken out of a Sow after she was killed," or "the penis of the possum which belonged to the Society and died Lately," both presented in 1709. But progress was made: membership more than doubled during his term in office and the ruinous finances of the Society were rescued and put on a firm footing.

Not Very Civil

Newton's presidency also had its dark side, however. He was dictatorial, high-handed, and self-serving. He packed the council with lackeys and used the Society as an instrument to pursue personal vendettas against Flamsteed and Leibniz. His authoritarian style was demonstrated in his handling of the Society's move to new premises in Crane Court off Fleet Street.

Now Sir Isaac (he had been knighted in April 1705), he convened a special meeting on September 16, 1710 to inform the council of his plans. An angry pamphlet from a disgruntled fellow reported that: "The President was not prepared ... to enter upon the debate but freely (though methinks not very civily) replied that he had good reasons for their removing which he did not think proper to be given there."

Old grudges died hard for Newton; the only known portrait of Hooke was mysteriously lost during the move.

MIXED RECEPTION

Exactly how Newton came to be president is not clear, but there is evidence that many of the fellows, perhaps aware of his difficult personality, were not thrilled. In order to be elected to the chair, Newton first had to be elected to the council, but around a fifth of the electors refused to vote for him for either post.

Crane Court, off Fleet Street, purchased at Newton's instigation (and insistence) as the first permanent home of the Royal Society.

To Explain the Properties of Light

NEWTON'S FIRST DISCOVERIES IN SCIENCE HAD BEEN IN THE FIELD OF OPTICS WITH HIS EXPERIMENTS ON LIGHT AND COLOR, BUT THE HARSH RESPONSE TO HIS THEORIES IN THE 1670S, AND IN PARTICULAR THE ATTACKS BY HOOKE, HAD DISSUADED HIM FROM PUBLISHING A FULL ACCOUNT. HOWEVER, OVER THE INTERVENING PERIOD NEWTON HAD AMASSED MORE EXPERIMENTAL EVIDENCE AND DELVED FURTHER INTO THE SECRETS OF NATURE; NOW HE WAS READY TO PRESENT HIS SECOND GREAT WORK.

Newton was entreated to release his full theory of light and color. John Wallis wrote, urging him to disclosure: "You say, you dare not publish it. And why not yet? Or, if not now, when then? You add, lest I create you some trouble. What trouble now, more then at another time? ... Meanwhile you lose the Reputation of it, and we the Benefit." He resisted for years, until 1703 brought an abrupt change of circumstance.

With Hooke safely in his grave and Newton pre-eminent at the Royal Society in his place, he wasted little time. *Opticks: or a Treatise on the Reflexions, Refractions, Inflexions and Colours of Light*, was presented to the council on February 16, 1704. "Mr Halley was desired to peruse it and give an abstract of it to the Society. The Society gave the President their thanks for the book and for his being pleased to publish it," the Journal Book recorded. "To avoid being engaged in Disputes about these Matters, I have hitherto delayed the Printing..." explained Newton in an "Advertisement" that served as a preface.

Better by Design

Opticks was a very different book from *Principia*. Written in English, it contained very little mathematics. Unlike its predecessor it was designed to be accessible, and this made it even more influential than the earlier work, especially when a Latin edition followed in 1706, allowing the book to be read across Europe. Primarily it was a narrative of experiments performed, theories formed and tested, and laws induced; effectively a handbook of the new experimental philosophy and thus one of the founding texts of science. Once again, Newton spelled out the difference between his work and all previous tomes on the topic: "My design in this book is not to explain the properties of light by hypotheses, but to propose and prove them by reason and experiments."

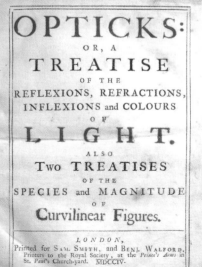

The frontispiece of the first edition of Newton's *Opticks*, published in 1704.

"My design in this book is not to explain the properties of light by hypotheses, but to propose and prove them by reason and experiments."

Dark rings caused where
peaks cancel troughs

Light rings where
amplitudes match

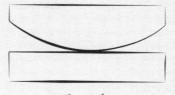

Convex glass on
flat glass

APPENDICES
**Appended to *Opticks* were
two mathematical papers,
"A Treatise on the Quadrature
of Curves" and "Enumeration
of the Lines of the Third
Order." Newton added these
partly to assert priority to the
discovery of the techniques
described in them (in the
light of the looming priority
dispute with Leibniz; see
page 136–7), and partly to
prove his credentials as a
great mathematician.**

Rainbows and Rings

The contents of *Opticks* were wonderfully wide-ranging, proving the scope and power of Newton's method. He began with refraction and reflection, discussed color and whiteness, and described his experiments with prisms, mirrors, and colored films (including the phenomena now known as "Newton's rings"). He showed how spectacles work. He explained the rainbow. He detailed the phenomenon known as interference; today this is described as the result of the wave-like nature of light, where peaks and troughs of light can "interfere" and cancel each other out, and this posed a real problem for Newton. He remained committed to the corpuscular theory of light, maintaining that rays of light are "very small Bodies emitted from shining Substances." To accommodate this he tried, unconvincingly, to explain interference as the result of light moving in "fits"; for example, "fits of easy transmission." Today science says that both views are accurate; light does behave like a wave, but Einstein showed that it also comes in tiny packets or quanta, called photons.

Above and Beyond

From purely optical phenomena the book expanded into whole new realms, covering biology and physiology, the working of the eye, sensation and metabolism in living creatures, electricity, friction, and putrefaction, and even cosmic speculations on the relationship between the divine and the material universe. His most advanced and speculative thoughts he segregated in a final section, a collection of rhetorical questions called the "Queries" (see pages 130–1).

Nineteenth-century
apparatus for demonstrating
Newton's rings.

Queries and Speculations

HAVING SPENT MOST OF HIS CAREER STUDIOUSLY OPPOSING "HYPOTHESES," IN THE "QUERIES" NEWTON GAVE FREE REIGN TO HIS SCIENTIFIC IMAGINATION. IN DOING SO HE PROVED HIMSELF TO BE BREATHTAKINGLY PRESCIENT, FOR THE "QUERIES" SEEM TO FORESHADOW MANY ASPECTS OF MODERN PHYSICS, FROM THE MECHANISM OF ELECTRICITY TO QUANTUM PHYSICS, FROM GRAVITATIONAL LENSING TO $E = MC^2$; THEY EVEN APPROACH THE UNIFIED THEORY OF NATURAL FORCES THAT REMAINS TO THIS DAY THE HOLY GRAIL OF PHYSICS.

Newton had originally considered a "Conclusio" to the *Principia* in which he would speculate about the mechanism of gravity and the possibility of a unified theory, but he had suppressed it, as he later suppressed a planned Book IV of the *Opticks*, which would have detailed similar speculations. Instead he added the "Queries" to Book III; 16 of them in the first edition, growing in number to 31 by the Latin edition of 1706. In them he explored a central tenet of his philosophy: nature was "consonant to herself"—governed by a small number of fundamental laws, which fit elegantly together to produce all the phenomena of the Universe.

Armed with this faith in nature, Newton was willing to speculate on apparently disparate fields. He considered electricity, posing the question: "Do not all bodies therefore abound with a very subtle, but active, potent electric spirit by which light is emitted, refracted, & reflected, electric attractions and fugations are performed...?" He speculated on the mechanism of gravity, and on whether occult forces governed light as they appeared to govern gravity.

Anticipating Einstein

Einstein's theory of relativity described how the fabric of space-time is distorted by gravity, and how this in turn causes light to bend around massive objects, such as stars—a phenomenon known as gravitational lensing; his theory was proved accurate in 1919. Yet Newton's very first Query: "Do not bodies act upon light at a distance, and by their action bend its rays; and is not action ... strongest at the least distance?" seems clearly to anticipate this phenomenon.

In Query V, Newton asked, "Do not bodies and light mutually act upon one another?", in a passage that can be read as anticipating another of Einstein's discoveries, the photoelectric effect, which laid the foundations for quantum mechanics. Query XXX reads very much like a description of Einstein's famous equation, $e = mc^2$, describing the equivalence

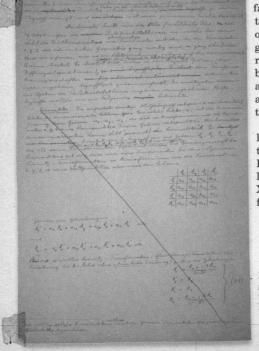

Einstein's manuscript for his paper on the general theory of relativity, which describes the geometry of space-time and builds on the Newtonian description of gravity.

and interchangeability of matter and energy: "Are not gross Bodies and Light convertible into one another? ... The changing of Bodies into Light, and Light into Bodies, is very conformable to the Course of Nature, which seems delighted with Transmutations."

Unified Theory

Newton's ultimate goal in the *Principia* had been to derive a theory that unified the macroscopic scale of the stars and planets with the microscopic scale of the chemicals in his alchemist's crucible. He had been unable to prove such a theory, but in his final Query he described his thinking on the matter:

"Have not the small Particles of Bodies certain Powers, Virtues or Forces, by which they act at a distance, not only upon the Rays of Light for reflecting, refracting, and inflecting them, but also upon one another for producing a great part of the Phænomena of Nature? For it's well known, that Bodies act one upon another by the Attractions of Gravity, Magnetism and Electricity; and these Instances shew the Tenor and Course of Nature, and make it not improbable but that there may be more attractive Powers than these. For Nature is very consonant and conformable to her self."

This passage has been interpreted as describing how atoms attract and interact with each other (the theory of chemical valencies), possibly even foreshadowing the discovery of subatomic forces such as nuclear forces and electrostatic energy; in other words, anticipating much of the modern model of physics.

A 2002 image from NASA's Hubble Space Telescope shows light from background galaxies distorted into arcs by the gravity of the cluster of yellow galaxies.

AMMUNITION
In the "Queries" Newton's speculations extend to the realm of the metaphysical; for example, in a passage where he described "Infinite Space" as the "Sensorium" of God. This was a reference to his esoteric theories about how the material and spiritual were related, and how God was active in the Universe. But such speculations made him vulnerable to the disputation he so dreaded, and indeed they did provide ammunition for Leibniz to pass scathing judgment on Newton as a philosopher: "This man has little success with Metaphysics."

"In this third Book I have only begun the Analysis of what remains to be discover'd ... hinting several things about it, and leaving the Hints to be examin'd and improved by the farther Experiments and Observations of such as are inquisitive." — NEWTON, OPTICKS

Falling Out with the Astronomer Royal

NEWTON'S CAREFUL STEWARD-
SHIP OF THE ROYAL SOCIETY
WAS MARRED BY HIS DESIRE
FOR UNCHALLENGED CONTROL,
AND BY THE BITTER FEUDS
HE CARRIED ON AGAINST ANY
SCIENTISTS WHO DARED TO
STAND UP TO HIM. A TYPICAL
EXAMPLE WAS HIS LONG
CONFLICT WITH THE FIRST
ASTRONOMER ROYAL, JOHN
FLAMSTEED. ALTHOUGH
THE TWO MEN HAD MUCH IN
COMMON, THEIR DIFFICULT
PERSONALITIES SAW THEM
LOCK HORNS FOR MORE
THAN 20 YEARS, BLIGHTING
FLAMSTEED'S CAREER.

A diagram from the *Principia*
showing the orbit of the comet of
1680 around the Sun—nothing
like this had ever been seen in
print before.

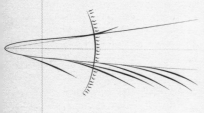

As with his former nemesis Hooke, Flamsteed and Newton had much common ground. From humble backgrounds—Flamsteed's father was a tradesman—both had risen by talent, hard work, and force of will to become leading natural philosophers. Both men had suffered the loss of maternal attachment in their early years and resented their stepparents—Flamsteed's mother had died when he was three and he never forgave his father for remarrying.

Flamsteed developed a passion for astronomy in his teens, and his diligence and expertise made him the premier stargazer in England, talents that were recognized when Charles II created the post of Astronomer Royal for him in 1675. The king commissioned Wren to design the handsome Royal Observatory on a hill in Greenwich, but shortage of funds meant the building was little more than a shell. Flamsteed had to provide his own instruments and hire assistants while scratching around to make a living, but over the next 15 years nonetheless managed to build up one of the greatest bodies of astronomical observations yet assembled.

The Year of Two Comets

The first correspondence between the two men dates to the early 1680s when Flamsteed wrote through a friend to suggest that two comets seen in a month in late 1680 might in fact be a single one, traveling to and then returning from the Sun, as if attracted and then repelled by a great magnet. Newton replied, objecting that the Sun, which he represented in his writing by the symbol ☉, could not be magnetic because it "is a vehemently hot body & magnetick bodies when made red hot lose their virtue."

Instead he sketched a diagram showing the comet approaching the Sun and traveling all the way around it before returning, admitting, "I can easily allow an attractive power in the ☉ whereby the Planets are kept in their courses about him from going away in tangent lines." Predating the *Principia* by seven years, this was the plainest statement so far of his concept of a gravitational force causing planets to veer off from their tangents.

The Most Exact Observer

In 1694 Newton, seeking to make the centerpiece of a planned second edition of the *Principia* a new "theory of the Moon"—a complete elucidation of the orbit of the Moon using the orbital mechanics he had laid out in the first edition—turned to the Astronomer Royal. He needed detailed observations of the lunar orbit as raw material for his calculations, and only Flamsteed had data of high enough quality. Newton began with flat-

Astronomers making observations at the Royal Observatory using a quadrant and a telescope, while a third man notes down their readings.

"I want not your calculations but your observations only... If you like this proposal, then pray send me first your observations... But if you like it not ... let me know plainly that I must be content to lose all the time & pains I have hitherto taken about the Moon's theory..."

— **NEWTON TO FLAMSTEED, 1694**

tery: "… for your observations to come abroad thus with a theory which you ushered into the world … would be much more for their advantage & your reputation than to keep them private… For such a theory will be a demonstration of their exactness and make you readily acknowledged the most exact observer that has hitherto appeared in the world."

Things soon started to go wrong, however. Although Flamsteed was an astronomer of precision and brilliance, his assistants were less competent, and he himself was overworked and underpaid. Mistakes crept into the data he was sending; Newton responded critically, but demanded still more data. Flamsteed made a cardinal error, daring to perform some calculations of his own and sending the results, rather than the raw data. Unfortunately he or one of his assistants made an error. Newton's response (above) was coldly dismissive, prompting Flamsteed to complain in his journal that the great scientist was "hasty, artificial, unkind, arrogant." Their feud had begun, and before it was done it would threaten to consume Flamsteed's life's work.

The Battle for the Star Catalog

NEWTON'S GROWING POWER WITHIN THE SCIENTIFIC ESTABLISHMENT EXACERBATED HIS RUTHLESS HOUNDING OF FLAMSTEED. HE USED HIS VICE-LIKE GRIP OVER THE ROYAL SOCIETY AND HIS INFLUENCE AT COURT TO PURSUE THE RAW DATA HE WAS CONVINCED FLAMSTEED POSSESSED, EMPLOYING EVERY WEAPON AT HIS DISPOSAL FROM SLY INGENUITY TO OUTRIGHT BULLYING. THE ASTRONOMER ROYAL BRAVELY DEFIED HIM TO THE END, WINNING A HOLLOW VICTORY AT GREAT PERSONAL COST.

Like Newton, Flamsteed hated to publish his work until he was satisfied that it was complete and unimpeachable; indeed, he believed his task as Astronomer Royal was not to release data piecemeal, but guard it jealously until he was ready to produce his masterwork, a catalog of the heavens, giving the positions and motions of all the celestial objects to a greater degree of precision than had ever been achieved. This put him on a collision course with Newton, who believed that Flamsteed's job was merely to feed him the data that he needed for his calculations. Infuriated by Flamsteed's refusal to play along, he hatched a scheme to force his hand.

A Royal Commission

Queen Anne's husband, Prince George, though noted for his stupidity, had pretensions to science, particularly astronomy. Through his contacts at court, Newton in 1705 prompted the prince to commission a great star catalog from the Astronomer Royal, to be entitled *Historia Cœlestis Britannica* (*A British History of the Heavens*). Flamsteed could not turn down such a commission, and Newton further engineered it that the Royal Society would oversee production of the volume.

Flamsteed was dismayed, even more so when he learned that the editorial committee appointed by the Society was

Queen Anne, who reigned from 1702 to 1714, and her husband Prince George. It was a sign of Newton's eminence that he enjoyed regular audiences with the royal couple.

"...honest Sir Isaac Newton (to use his own words) would have all things in his own power, to spoil or sink them; that he might force me to second his designs and applaud him, which no honest man would do nor could do; and, God be thanked, I lay under no necessity of doing."

— Flamsteed, suppressed preface to the 1725 edition of *Historia Cœlestis*

packed with Newton's lackeys, noting that, "With these persons Isaac Newton began to act his part, and carry on his designs." Determined to frustrate him, Flamsteed delayed publication in every way possible. Newton wrote in cold fury: "[if] you propose anything else or make any excuses or unnecessary delays it will be taken for an indirect refusal to comply with Her Majesty's order. Your speedy & direct answer & compliance is expected."

Showdown at the Society

Matters came to a head when Flamsteed ignored a direct order to report observations of a solar eclipse. On October 26, 1711, he was hauled before the council of the Royal Society, presided over by Newton himself. Flamsteed recorded the explosive meeting that followed: "...all he said was in a rage: he called me many hard names; puppy was the most innocent of them... I only desired to keep his temper, restrain his passion, and thanked him as often as he gave me ill names..."

Inexorably Newton exerted his will. In 1712 a first edition of the *Historia Cœlestis*, under the editorship of Newton's protégé Halley—a man for whom Flamsteed had a particular loathing (calling him a "lazy and malicious thief")—was finally produced. In 1713 Newton was able to publish his lunar theory in a second edition of the *Principia*, from which he erased practically every mention of Flamsteed. But the Astronomer Royal eventually achieved a small victory over the man he called "sly Newton."

With the death of Queen Anne in 1714, and of his ally Lord Halifax (the ennobled Montagu) a year later, Newton's influence at court declined. In 1715 Flamsteed was given leave to collect almost all copies of the "corrupted and spoiled" *Historia Cœlestis* and "made a sacrifice of them to heavenly truth," burning them in the grounds of the Royal Observatory. In 1725, six years after his death, the catalog was finally published in the form he had dreamt of; but its preface, a scathing attack on Newton accusing him of "disingenuous and malicious practices" and "cunning forecasts," was suppressed for over a century.

The frontispiece of the *Historia Cœlestis*, with a portrait of Flamsteed wreathed in glory.

Clash of the Titans

IF THERE WAS ONE MAN IN EUROPE CAPABLE OF CONTENDING FOR NEWTON'S INTELLECTUAL CROWN, IT WAS GERMAN POLYMATH GOTTFRIED WILHELM VON LEIBNIZ. EXPERTS NOW AGREE THAT BOTH MEN ARRIVED AT THE INVENTION OF CALCULUS INDEPENDENTLY, BUT NEWTON WAS INCAPABLE OF SHARING CREDIT. ASSUMING THAT LEIBNIZ HAD PLAGIARIZED HIM, HE AND HIS SUPPORTERS ENGAGED IN A DECADES-LONG FEUD WITH FAR-REACHING CONSEQUENCES FOR BRITISH SCIENCE.

Born in Leipzig in 1646, Leibniz trained as a lawyer, served as a diplomat and administrator, and made groundbreaking contributions to theology and philosophy, but his great passion was for science and mathematics. In 1673 he visited London to present a calculating machine he had built with his own hands, and was elected as a fellow of the Royal Society. Although he did not meet Newton, he did make the acquaintance of the mathematician-publisher John Collins.

Contributions and Controversy

Returning to Paris, Leibniz spent the next two years engaged in mathematical discoveries that rivaled Newton's own *anni mirabiles* during the plague years. By 1675 he had independently arrived at theories of infinite series and infinitesimal calculus, taking great care to devise a system of notation that could be easily understood and used by other mathematicians, in contrast to Newton, who had made no effort to make his unwieldy theory of fluxions accessible to others.

From Paris Leibniz had corresponded with Collins in London, who had sent him news (though not specifics) of advances in mathematics including mention of Newton, while during a 1677 visit to London Collins allowed him access to papers and correspondence. These incidents would provide the grounds for later accusations of plagiarism, although analysis of Leibniz's notes and process show that his advances were made independently.

In 1676, at the prompting of Collins and Oldenburg, who suspected a looming controversy, Newton had written to Leibniz summarizing his discoveries in infinite series and alluding to his "method of fluxions." Nervous of intellectual

Leibniz's calculating machine. His major advance was the use of a stepped drum—a cylinder bearing nine teeth of different lengths that increase in equal amounts around the drum—a principle used in calculating machines up until the 20th century.

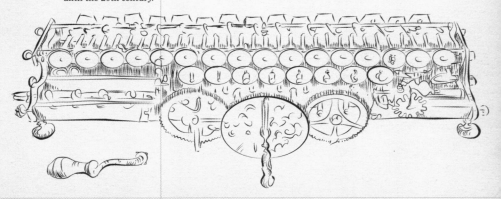

theft, Newton encoded the basic principle of his method in an encrypted sentence regarded as an early form of patent: "I cannot proceed with the explanation of the fluxions now, I have preferred to conceal it thus: 6acc dae13eff7i3l9n4o4qrr4s8t12vx." (Decrypted, this translates to a Latin phrase meaning: "Given an equation involving any number of fluent quantities, to find the fluxions: and vice versa.")

Newton included a covering note: "I hope this will so far satisfy M. Leibniz that it will not be necessary for me to write any more…" But the matter would not rest. In 1684 Leibniz published his first paper on calculus, and his version quickly became the standard in continental Europe. Blithely unaware of how this would sit with Newton, he wrote to a friend in July of that year: "I acknowledge that Mr. Newton already had the principles … but one does not come upon all the results at one time; one man makes one contribution, another man another."

Breaking Leibniz's Heart

The controversy escalated until, in 1712, an outraged Leibniz wrote to the Royal Society demanding an apology. Newton seized his chance, convening a supposedly objective committee to investigate the dispute. In practice he chose the members and wrote the report (known as the "Commercium Epistolicum") himself. The verdict was predictably one-sided.

In 1713 Newton went further still, penning an "Account of the Commercium Epistolicum" that descended into personal attacks and character assassination. In 1715 the new king, George of Hanover, who happened to be Leibniz's employer, asked Newton to write a letter of apology, but, never one to give up a grudge easily, the bitter scientist simply reiterated that the German was "guilty of calumny."

By this time Leibniz was isolated and ill; he died in late 1716, yet Newton was vengeful still. He deleted all mention of Leibniz from the third edition of the *Principia* in 1726 and in his last days boasted that he had "broke Leibniz's heart with his reply to him." Newton's victory was British science's loss; it was held back for decades, arguably centuries, by its refusal to accept the superior method and notation of Leibniz's calculus.

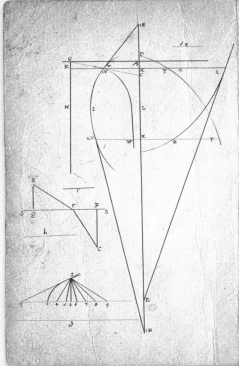

"In symbols," wrote Leibniz, "one observes an advantage in discovery which is greatest when they express the exact nature of a thing briefly and, as it were, picture it; then indeed the labor of thought is wonderfully diminished."

"Second inventors count for nothing."

— NEWTON IN HIS SECOND DRAFT OF

"ACCOUNT OF THE COMMERCIUM EPISTOLICUM"

CHAPTER SEVEN

THE
END OF
DAYS

The Books of Knowledge

NEWTON'S CAREER AS A
SCIENTIFIC EXPLORER WAS
EFFECTIVELY OVER BY THE
TIME *OPTICKS* WAS PUBLISHED,
BUT HE CONTINUED RESEARCH-
ING AND WRITING INTO THE
LAST YEARS OF HIS LIFE. THE
TOPIC THAT EXERCISED HIM UP
UNTIL THE END WAS THE STUDY
OF BIBLICAL HISTORY AND
PROPHECY. TO UNDERSTAND
WHAT DROVE HIM CEASELESSLY
TO REWORK TIMELINES OF
FUTURE EVENTS AND OBSESS
OVER THE EXACT PROPORTIONS
OF SOLOMON'S TEMPLE, IT IS
NECESSARY TO UNDERSTAND
THE CONTEXT OF THESE
PURSUITS.

The importance of the concept of the *prisca sapientia*, the primal wisdom, in the context of Newton's alchemy has already been explained (see page 76). But the *prisca sapientia* was just part of a larger picture. Today science is carried out within a generally non-religious, if not atheistic, context. In Newton's day it was exactly the opposite; everything Newton did was in the light of his religious belief and for the glory of God. More specifically, Newton and most of his contemporaries fervently believed that nature was a great work of God, and that it was their duty to understand it, and by doing so to reconstitute it.

The Book of Nature

"In the beginning was the Word, and the Word was with God, and the Word was God." These words were taken literally by the scholars of Newton's era. It was accepted as a basic truth that God had created the universe via language and that the original, Adamic language (the language spoken by Adam before the Fall) would thus constitute the code for Creation. It was literally the language in which the "book of nature" was written, and nature was explicitly seen as a great book. The goal of the natural philosopher was to read the book of nature, but this was difficult for several reasons.

Firstly, the Fall of humankind had disturbed the perfect order of the Edenic world, and ever since the book of nature had been degrading. The very act of recovering it and thus reconstituting it as it was originally written by God would help to reverse this corruption and help to make restitution for the

sins of humankind. Secondly, the language of creation was a great cipher, a complex code in need of decipherment. Galileo Galilei had asserted that the book of nature was written in the language of mathematics with characters that were geometric in form. Newton's pursuit of a mathematical philosophy of nature was thus his attempt to decode this language.

A pilgrim peers through the curtain of nature to view the secret workings of the cosmos; similarly, Newton sought to read the design of God in the book of nature.

"Philosophers have hitherto attempted the search of Nature in vain; but I hope the principles here laid down will afford some light either to this or some truer method of philosophy."

— NEWTON'S PREFACE TO THE FIRST EDITION OF *PRINCIPIA*

The Book of Scripture

Alongside the book of nature, one of the other manifestations of God's creative power was the book of scripture, in which scholars could discern the code of creation from the divinely inspired word, so that religious enquiry offered another route to truth. Just as alchemy and natural philosophy sought to read the book of nature and in doing so recover the *prisca sapientia*, so through theology, and particularly the branches of inquiry that Newton pursued in his later years, the scholar could seek to recover the *prisca theologia*, the ancient and perfect religion. This achievement would mean nothing less than the dawning of a new Jerusalem, a world in which all would live in harmony and in perfect knowledge of nature and God.

The Power of Prophecy

As well as the roots of the Trinitarianism Newton despised so much, his early theological researches had also concentrated on prophecy, particularly the Book of Revelation and the Book of Daniel. As parts of the book of scripture these were nothing less than clues from God about the story of Creation; the history of the world encoded, available to those who could decipher it, or more specifically to those who could reconstitute the original, true version of scripture from the version corrupted from over a millennium of translation, transcription, and, according to Newton, the deliberate perversions of the Catholics and the Trinitarians. Accordingly Newton engaged in exhaustive research to trace the history of scripture and theology, and in order to match prophecy with history, and thus decode it, he labored over the chronologies of ancient kingdoms.

Michelangelo's *Last Judgment*, the day that Newton perhaps believed he could help to bring about through his researches.

The Bible Code

FOR NEWTON THE BIBLE WAS PROPHECY; ITS DIVINE SIGNIFICANCE LAY NOT IN THE REVELATION OF TRUTHS ABOUT ETERNAL LIFE SO MUCH AS THE ENCRYPTED GUIDE TO HUMAN HISTORY, PAST AND FUTURE, WHICH IT CONSTITUTED. UNPICKING THE COMPLEX WEAVE OF THE PROPHECIES WAS, HE WROTE, "NO IDLE SPECULATION, NO MATTER OF INDIFFERENCY BUT A DUTY OF THE GREATEST MOMENT," ESSENTIAL PREPARATION FOR THE SECOND COMING AND THE END OF DAYS.

"Having searched after knowledge in the prophetic scriptures, I have thought my self bound to communicate it for the benefit of others... For I am persuaded that this will prove of great benefit to those who ... desire to go on unto perfection..."

— NEWTON'S INTRODUCTION TO OBSERVATIONS UPON THE PROPHECIES

If prophecy was the essence of the Bible, the Revelation of St. John was the key text. "There is no book in all the scriptures so much recommended & guarded by providence as this," he wrote, and a discourse on Revelation was one of the first theological writings he produced in the 1670s. He revised it constantly thereafter and it may well have been the last thing he was working on before he died. Yet despite his avowal that, "Having searched after knowledge in the prophetic scriptures, I have thought my self bound to communicate it for the benefit of others," the road to eventual publication of his theories and deductions was long and torturous, culminating only in posthumous publication.

The Parts of Prophecy

Initially Newton's interest in the prophecies was linked to his Arianism, for he believed that his work would help others to understand the one, true form of religion—in other words, his own—when it was finally revealed at the time of the Second Coming. But in order to decode the prophecies and predict the actual date of the Second Coming, it was essential to know which of the prophesied events had already happened, how long they had taken, and how this corresponded with the time scale laid out in Revelation. This then, was where the study of prophecy intersected with the study of history. Newton plunged into both wholesale.

He approached the deciphering of prophecy with the same rigorous analytical method that he applied to his studies of natural philosophy. He believed that just as nature was harmonious and "consonant with herself," so the different parts of scripture also harmonized with one another. "For the parts of Prophesy are like the separated parts of a Watch. They appear confused & must be compared & put together before they can be useful, & those parts are certainly to be put together which fit without straining."

The End Is Nigh-ish

The generally accepted Protestant interpretation of the prophecies was that the "great apostasy" described in Revelation was the emergence of the Catholic Church c.400 CE, and that this could be used as a starting point from which to apply the rest of the chronology laid out in the book. It was also generally accepted that the Second Coming, the destruction of the Antichrist, and the dawning of the Millennium (the thousand-year rule of the new Messiah) were set by prophecy to occur 1260 years after the great apostasy, and that this therefore set the date of the Second Coming at around the mid-17th century.

Many Protestants of the period confidently expected the Second Coming at any moment.

Newton was more circumspect, because he had a different, and to mainstream Anglicans, heretical view of what constituted the great apostasy. As an Arian he dated this event to the antics of Athanasius and the triumph of Trinitarianism. Having thus obtained an unorthodox starting point for dating the prophecies, he then worked out an increasingly complex interpretation of the timescales leading up to and away from this point.

What date did Newton set? His complex chronology of the history of the Church equated the start of the crucial 1260-year period with the early seventh century (to which he ascribed the date of the breaking of the fourth seal as described in Revelation), and thus forecast the Second Coming for the 19th century. Later he would revise this to 1948.

Newton spent the rest of his life successively revising his interpretations, and with each revision he took pains to obscure further the Arianism that had originally guided him. When a version of his discourse on the prophecies was eventually published as *Observations upon the Prophecies* shortly after his death, it proved to be rambling, pointless, and quite impenetrable, giving little hint of the extraordinarily ambitious agenda that had inspired its earlier drafts.

"And I looked, and beheld a pale horse: and his name that sat on him was Death, and Hell followed with him. And power was given unto them over the fourth part of the earth, to kill with sword, and with famine, and with plague, and with the wild beasts of the earth."

— REVELATION 6:8

St. John having his vision of the four horsemen of the apocalypse. Newton expected their arrival in 1948.

The Millennium Project

As he looked forward to the End of Days, so Newton also took past history as his preserve, applying his formidable scholarship to the forensic reconstruction of primitive, antediluvian Christianity, which he believed to be the root of all other religions and civilizations. His interest was not simply academic; it formed part of a larger project of almost inconceivable scope.

Caroline of Brandenburg-Ansbach, Princess of Wales, a cultured, intelligent woman who took an interest in Newton's research.

Beginning in the 1670s, Newton had developed a "Discourse on the origins of religion among the gentiles" (in other words, the ancient non-Jewish peoples, from the Egyptians and Babylonians to the Greeks and Romans), which explained how all the other ancient religions and civilizations were corrupted and confused versions of the original, true religion, versions created by the descendants of Noah after the Flood as they spread out to repopulate the world. He explained at great length how the gods of the Egyptians, Greeks, and other ancients were simply mythologized versions of ancient kings and heroes, relating, for instance, the 12 major gods of the ancient gentiles to the 12 tribes of Israel from which he believed all the gentiles descended.

Chronology of Ancient Kingdoms

In the 1690s he began to revise this discourse, but resisted publication until, in 1716, the Princess of Wales asked him for a copy. Reluctantly he reworked it into an "Abstract"; only many years later would he come to publish a very large and much revised version as the *Chronology of Ancient Kingdoms Amended*. He died while still engaged in revising it, but John Conduitt published the full volume the year after, in 1728.

His original intent had been to lay out his theories about the nature of the true religion of the time of Noah, before the Biblical Flood, but these would have been extremely radical and unorthodox. So he suppressed any hint of unorthodoxy and produced, instead, a book that was, like the *Observations*, both confused and rambling. Westfall describes it as: "A work of colossal tedium... It is read today only by the tiniest remnant who for their sins must pass through its purgatory."

Ultimate Ambition

Why did Newton devote so much time and energy to these apparently fruitless researches into prophecy and ancient history? What was his motivation? The study of the End Times is known as "eschatology," and men like Newton pursued it not simply for academic purposes. They believed that successful reconstruction of the ancient primitive religion of Noah and of Adam before him, along with perfect decryption of the prophecies, could actually affect the fate of the universe.

Henry More (1614–87), the Cambridge Platonist, an alumnus of Newton's old school in Grantham who was a great influence on the younger man.

The first flush of theological research inspired in Newton the same kind of ecstasy of discovery as the natural philosophical breakthroughs of the plague years. The Cambridge philosopher Henry More was a major influence on his approach to prophecy, and his account of Newton's reaction to his "Exposition of the Apocalypse" gives a clear picture of the intensity with which the young scholar approached his task:

"he seem'd to me ... (by the manner of his countenance which is ordinarily melancholy and thoughtful, but then mighty lightsome and cheerful, and by the free profession of what satisfaction he took therein) to be in a manner transported."

Newton was prepared to go to any lengths to achieve this, pursuing his goal through mathematical, experimental, philosophical, alchemical, and theological means. According to Betty Jo Teeter Dobbs, the pre-eminent scholar of Newton's esoteric occupations, the eschatological agenda he pursued extended as far as the question, "Will the rediscovery of the pure, potent fire that is the ultimate secret of the active alchemical principle lead to the restoration of true religion and the ushering in of the millennium [the thousand-year reign of Christ on Earth]?" In other words, could his various researches actually bring about the Second Coming?

Messiah Complex

What does this extraordinary ambition say about Newton's self-image? Clues are scattered throughout his writings to suggest that it was somewhat inflated. For instance, he believed that the prophecies were intended for, and could only be understood by, the adherents of the true Church. These adherents were, he wrote, "but a remnant, a few scattered persons which God hath chosen, such as ... can set themselves sincerely & earnestly to search after the truth." As an Arian, there is no question but that Newton believed himself to be one of those few "which God hath chosen." Elsewhere it is evident that he identified with Biblical and historical figures: for instance, with Arius and with the prophet Elijah. How far did he carry his interpretations and identifications? Did he believe that it was significant that he had been born on Christmas Day, with a father up in heaven?

"This religion was easily understood by the meanest of the people & was handed down amongst them by tradition in simplicity until men skilled in the learning of heathens Cabbalists & Schoolmen corrupted it with metaphysicks..."

— NEWTON, "DRAFTS ON THE HISTORY OF THE CHURCH"

Rebuilding the Temple

ONE OF THE MOST INTRIGUING OFFSHOOTS OF NEWTON'S THEOLOGICAL RESEARCH WAS HIS OBSESSION WITH THE FLOOR PLAN OF THE TEMPLE OF SOLOMON. HE BELIEVED THIS BUILDING REPRESENTED THE PERFECT HARMONY BETWEEN THE PRIMITIVE, ORIGINAL RELIGION AND THE PERFECT KNOWLEDGE OF NATURE POSSESSED BY ITS PRACTITIONERS. HIS CONCEPT OF THE TEMPLE, AND PARTICULARLY ITS CENTRAL FEATURE, THE PRYTANEUM, HAS BEEN CREDITED AS AN INSPIRATION FOR HIS CONCEPT OF GRAVITY.

In the late 1670s Newton began what was intended to be a multi-volume history of the Church, which he continued on and off until the end of his life. Book VIII was to illustrate how divine prophecy was fulfilled and thus validated by the history of the Church, including its prehistory. Accordingly, he immersed himself in the history and practice of ancient Judaism, which he saw as a "type": a sort of prototype set up by God to instruct, with the aid of prophecy, what came after—"God forecast everything of great moment first by types and then explained those types by new prophecies." The practices of ancient Judaism and the prophecies of Revelation were "like twin prophecies of the same things," he explained, which "mutually explicate each other and cannot be satisfactorily understood apart from one another."

Blueprint

Study of ancient Judaism led him to consider the works of Solomon, the Jewish king he regarded as perhaps the greatest of ancient philosophers and alchemists, and in particular his mighty Temple, its dimensions and layout ordained by God. He believed that the plan of the Temple had spiritual and occult significance. It was a physical representation of the universe and all its secret laws, which were encoded within its proportions: "Temples were anciently contrived to represent the frame of the Universe as the true Temple of the great God." Newton learned Hebrew so that he could read the original Old Testament books that described the floor plan of the Temple, in particular verses from the Book of Ezekiel. Working through Ezekiel he produced detailed annotations to the text, together with a comprehensive floor plan.

The Prytaneum

In this Temple the different aspects of God's creativity came together: "Now the rationale of this institution was that the God of Nature should be worshipped in a temple which imitates Nature, in a temple which is, as it were, a reflection of God. Everyone agrees that a Sanctum with a fire in the middle was an emblem of the system of the world…"

"This structure commends itself by the utmost simplicity and harmony of all its proportions."

— NEWTON, "DRAFTS ON THE HISTORY OF THE CHURCH"

Newton called this inner sanctum the Prytaneum, and explained that its layout was a
representation of the cosmos, particularly
the true heliocentric "frame of the world."
"The whole heavens they reckoned to be the
true and real temple of God & therefore that
a Prytaneum might deserve the name of his
Temple they framed it so as in the fittest
manner to represent the whole system of the
heavens." Accordingly it had a central fire,
around which were arranged lamps representing the planets.

Back to the Future

Newton regarded the temples of other faiths
and civilizations, and even the churches of
his own time, as debased copies of the
original, pure model. He saw a direct link
between on the one hand the corruption of
natural philosophy and the degradation of
the book of nature, and on the other the
corruption of the form of the temple in which
God was worshiped.

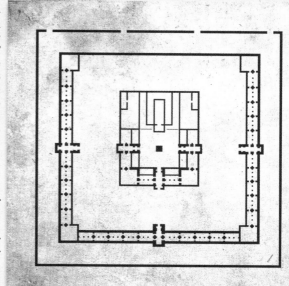

Newton drew up a detailed
plan of the Temple of
Solomon, believing its
proportions encoded sacred
truths about the structure
of the Universe.

   Restoring one could help with the restoration of the other.
Newton would attempt both: by reconstituting the exact dimensions of the Temple he might create a roadmap for the perfection of natural philosophy, while through his natural philosophy,
his optics, mathematics, and mechanics, he was attempting to
achieve this perfection directly, and perhaps thereby restore
original, pure, and true religion.

   What seem to modern observers to be wildly disparate
pursuits—one the epitome of science, the other the eccentrici-
ties of a deluded crank—were actually simply two sides of the
same coin for Newton. Understanding this central point—that
for Newton the different
strands of his research
were simply facets of a
much larger whole—is
key to understanding
the scope and grandeur
of his whole project.

A contemporary
interpretation of what the
Temple of Solomon, atop
the Temple Mount, might
have looked like.

Family Matters

ABANDONED AS A SMALL CHILD, SENT AWAY TO SCHOOL AS A TEENAGER, A SOLITARY SCHOLAR AT CAMBRIDGE, AND A CONFIRMED BACHELOR THROUGHOUT HIS LONG LIFE, NEWTON WAS FAR FROM BEING A FAMILY-ORIENTED MAN. YET IN LATER LIFE HE CAME TO ENJOY THE ROLE OF PATRIARCH TO HIS EXTENDED FAMILY, AND WITH THE ARRIVAL OF HIS NIECE, CATHERINE BARTON, AS HIS HOUSEKEEPER, HE DEVELOPED PERHAPS HIS ONLY LASTING RELATIONSHIP WITH A WOMAN.

Despite his personal asceticism and puritan values, and his ferocity in defense of the nation's money supply, Newton could be generous and indulgent, especially to family members. Although he had no full brothers or sisters and no children of his own, his half-siblings and Ayscough cousins from his mother's family ensured that he had a large number of relatives, mostly poor and needy. He was often happy to help them out, which he could afford to do, having added to the considerable fortune he inherited from his mother through his exertions at the Mint.

Humility and Honor

After his nephew Robert was killed in Canada, he spent £4,000 purchasing an estate for his widow and children. He handed out sums of £500, £100, and £800 to various Ayscoughs. After receiving a begging letter from the daughter of his uncle, Katherine Rastall ("Sir, I humbly desire you that you will be pleased to give … something for me… Sir, humbly begging the favour that you will be pleased to answer this I remain sir your humble servant."), he duly sent her money. He was even generous to minor acquaintances, as evidenced by a letter he received from Mary Davies in 1723: "Honoured Sir, I have made bold to trouble your honour with these few lines to return your honour thanks for the two guineas that your honour was pleased to send us…"

Full Fraught with Beauty

The most significant member of Newton's family was his niece, Catherine Barton, daughter of his half-sister Hannah Smith and brother to the nephew who died in Canada. She came to London to keep house for Newton, probably some time around 1696 when she was just 17. By this time Newton had moved out of his cramped quarters in the Tower to a house in Jermyn Street. To beauty and intelligence she added the vivacity of a country girl, and she succeeded in winning the heart of both her uncle and many others. A Frenchman who came to a dinner party at Newton's house waxed lyrical: "Ever since I beheld her I have adored her not only for her great beauty but for her lively and refined wit."

"I had your two letters & am glad the air agrees with you, & though the fever is loath to leave you yet I hope it abates… Your very loving Uncle"

— WRITING TO CATHERINE IN 1700 TO ENQUIRE AFTER HER RECOVERY FROM SMALLPOX

Newton's house on
St. Martin's Street in
London, where he lived
from September 1710
until May 1722.

Eventually she would become a great society beauty, close friends with Jonathan Swift, the author and satirist, and the lover of Newton's friend and political ally Lord Halifax, the chancellor of the exchequer. He toasted her in rhyme during a dinner at the Kit Kat Club in 1703, describing her as "full fraught with beauty." Their relationship caused something of a scandal at the time, and it was mistakenly claimed that Newton owed his appointment at the Mint to her influence on Halifax. Voltaire, despite being a great fan of Newton, wrote that, "The infinitesimal calculus and gravity would have availed nothing without a pretty niece." In practice Newton had secured the position of master before Catherine even arrived in London.

John Conduitt

Halifax died in 1715, and two years later an army officer, John Conduitt, who had recently made an archaeological discovery in Spain, came to Newton's house. There he met Catherine, ten years his senior, and just a few weeks later they were married. Conduitt was a keen disciple of his new uncle, and recorded their conversations and collected notes toward a planned biography. Although he never wrote it, the material he compiled provides the basis for much of what is known of Newton's life. Catherine moved in with her new husband, but the couple continued to care for Newton throughout his final years, and Conduitt eventually succeeded him at the Mint.

DOUBLE STANDARDS?
Newton's biographers have struggled to reconcile his devout Puritanism and censorious sexual mores with his apparent approval of or at least tacit complicity in the affair between Catherine and Halifax, which was an open secret. A psychoanalytic interpretation is that by facilitating a sexual liaison between a female relative and his friend he was vicariously acting out a subconscious desire to make love to his mother. Or it could be that Catherine and Halifax were common-law man and wife and that Newton recognized this bond.

The Final Years

**NEWTON LIVED TO BE 84
AND RETAINED ENOUGH OF
HIS FACULTIES TO BE WORKING
UP UNTIL THE END. THE YEARS
OF HIS CREATIVITY WERE LONG
BEHIND HIM, BUT NEWTON
STEWARDED HIS LEGACY AND
CONTINUED TO REVISE HIS
CHRONOLOGIES. BY THE
TIME OF HIS DEATH HE WAS
ACCOUNTED ONE OF THE
GREAT ORNAMENTS OF THE
NATION, AND AFFORDED A
GRAND STATE BURIAL IN
WESTMINSTER ABBEY,
POSSIBLY THE FIRST MAN TO
HAVE BEEN SO HONORED FOR
HIS INTELLECTUAL ACHIEVE-
MENTS ALONE.**

Several anecdotes survive of Newton's declining years, but many of them derive from those close to him who worshiped at his altar, and can hardly be accounted non-partisan. Conduitt was joined as chief cheerleader by the physician and antiquarian William Stukeley, who came from the same part of the country as Newton. The two became friends, and when Stukeley moved back to Grantham he made a concerted effort to gather anecdotes from the locals about the early life of his hero, which would prove to be another valuable resource for later biographers.

Neither Stiff nor Elated

Conduitt recorded that in his later years Newton was plump but retained "a very lively piercing eye," a full head of snow-white hair, and all his teeth but one (remarkable for a man with such a long history of working with mercury). He insisted that the old man displayed "an innate modesty and simplicity" and that "he was blessed with a very happy and vigorous constitution." However, not everyone agreed. Thomas Hearne described him as "of no promising Aspect... He was full of thought, and spoke very little in company, so that his conversation was not agreeable..."

Stukeley was stung by Humphrey Newton's assertion that he had only ever seen his master laugh once (see page 59), but

William Stukeley (1687–1765), antiquary and collector of Newtonian anecdotes.

even as he denied this humorlessness he affirmed it: "According to my own observations tho' Sir Isaac was of a very serious, & compos'd frame of mind, yet I have often seen him laugh ... in company he behaved very agreeably; courteous, affable, he was easily made to smile, if not to laugh." There were still flashes of the old temper. Stukeley reported that when he applied for the post of secretary to the Royal Society without first asking the president, "Sir Isaac showed a coolness towards me for 2 or 3 years."

Alongside his historical research, Newton oversaw further revised editions of his principal works, selecting young mathematician Henry Pemberton to edit the third edition of the *Principia*. Working with the 80-year-old Newton, Pemberton recorded that, "Though his memory was much decayed, I found he perfectly understood his own writings, contrary to what I had frequently heard in discourse from many persons. Neither his extreme great age, nor his universal reputation had rendered him stiff in opinion, or in any degree elated."

Much Failed

In spite of his age Newton continued to attend meetings of the Royal Society until ill health began to intervene. In his later years his focus drifted and he was liable to regale the assembly with tales of his Cambridge days, such as "a very remarkable Experiment he made formerly in Trinity Colledge Kitchin upon the heart of an Eel which he Cutt into three pieces … putting Spittle upon any of the Sections had no Effect…" He continued to give generously to charity and family. But his health declined steadily, his chief complaint being a bladder stone, which caused incontinence, and which together with gout confined him to what passed in the 18th century as a kind of wheelchair. He insisted on walking to church, nonetheless, stubbornly telling Conduitt, "use legs & have legs."

By early 1727 James Stirling found him "much failed and not able to do as he has done," yet he had strength enough to go into town with Conduitt (from lodgings he had taken up amidst the more salubrious airs of Kensington) in order to burn a pile of papers that may have included radical esoteric manuscripts. In mid-March he endured a bout of agony from the stone, and died a few days later on March 20, having refused to receive the Anglican sacrament, a last gesture toward his heavily concealed Arian beliefs. After a period of "lying in state" in Westminster Abbey, London, he was buried at a prominent spot in the nave, attended by several great nobles of the realm.

"March 23rd. 1727. The Chair being Vacant by the Death of Sir Isaac Newton there was no Meeting this Day."

— JOURNAL BOOK OF THE ROYAL SOCIETY

Westminster Abbey, where Newton's tomb is the center of a collection of memorials known as "Scientists' Corner."

NEWTON'S ESTATE

Newton died intestate, which occasioned much wrangling over his estate. An inventory revealed an enormous library of nearly 2,000 books, in addition to a stash of his own unpublished manuscripts. His liquid assets came to nearly £32,000, a considerable fortune at the time.

The baroque memorial of Newton's tomb, which shows him reclining on a pile of his own books.

Building the Myth of Newton

EVEN DURING HIS LIFETIME NEWTON'S ACOLYTES BEGAN TRANSFORMING THE MAN INTO MYTH. IN 1688 THE MARQUIS DE L'HÔPITAL HAD ASKED, "IS HE LIKE OTHER MEN?" NOW IT SEEMED THERE WAS A CONCERTED EFFORT TO PROVE THAT HE WAS NOT, THAT HE WAS A KIND OF SUPERMAN, EQUIPPED WITH GIFTS ALMOST DIVINE IN NATURE. HIS LEGACY WAS TO TRANSFORM BOTH SCIENCE AND THE WAY SCIENCE WAS SEEN.

Newton's rigid control of his own work and image, almost pathological aversion to controversy, dictatorial rule over the scientific establishment in Britain, and vocal band of cheerleaders all helped to ensure that his image was carefully manicured during his lifetime. Memoirs such as those written by Humphrey Newton, John Conduitt, and William Stukeley helped to cement that image after his death. According to Conduitt, for instance, "His whole life was one continued series of labour, patience, humility, temperance, meekness, humanity, beneficence & piety without any tincture of vice…" while Stukeley waxed lyrical about his death throes: "Such a struggle had his great soul… All this he bore with a most exemplary and remarkable patience, truly philosophical, truly Christian…"

Orations

In the years following his death Newton's stature continued to grow. He was seen as the philosopher of light and the standard bearer of the Enlightenment. Voltaire, a great popularizer of his in continental Europe, wrote: "The labyrinth and abyss of infinity is another new journey undertaken by Newton and he has given us a thread with which we can find our way through." Three years after the scientist's death, Alexander Pope was moved to pen the famous lines: "Nature and Nature's laws lay hid in night; God said, Let Newton be! And All was light."

The Power of Newton

Attempts were made to popularize the new philosophy. An Italian book rendered into English as *Sir Isaac Newton's Philosophy Explain'd for the Use of the Ladies* illustrated the inverse-square law by using it to calculate the power of attraction between separated lovers. But the main thrust was in the opposite direction, as Newtonianism was rapidly developed into a creed, asserting its power through demonstrations that seemed miraculous. Halley amazed the public with his prediction that the comet of 1682 would return every 76 years. In 1715 he used Newton's system to predict a total solar eclipse. Fellows of the Royal Society gathered to observe it, joined by a Muslim envoy from Tripoli (in modern-day Libya). William Whiston related his reaction:

"[He] at first thought we were distracted [deranged], by pretending to know so very punctually when God Almighty would totally eclipse the Sun; which his own mussulmen [Muslims] were not able to do… When the eclipse came exactly as we foretold, he was asked again, what he thought of the matter now? His answer was, that he supposed we knew this by art magick."

*Alexander Pope
(1688-1744)*

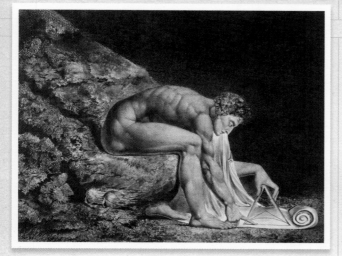

The artist and visionary William Blake depicted Newton engrossed in his geometry, blind to the creative possibilities of nature.

William Blake
(1757–1827)

The Backlash

Natural philosophy developed into science and Newtonianism increased its power and its scope; it desired to conquer the Universe. Pierre-Simon Laplace, known as the French Newton, declared that if the positions and forces of all things were known, and Newton's laws applied, "nothing would be uncertain, and the future, like the past, would be present to the eyes." Inevitably there was a backlash as Romantic poets like Shelley and Keats accused Newton of unweaving the rainbow. The visionary poet and artist William Blake saw him as a "dark Power," responsible for unleashing the "cogs tyrannic" of the Industrial Revolution.

Yet much of this stemmed from a false image of Newton, as his esoteric obsessions and religious unorthodoxy were suppressed in a kind of conspiracy of silence. In 1831 Newton's first great biographer, David Brewster, who had seen the unpublished manuscripts, was still able to insist: "There is no reason to suppose that Sir Isaac Newton was a believer in the doctrines of alchemy." It was not until his alchemical papers came into the possession of John Maynard Keynes, in the 1930s, that his true identity emerged: "Isaac Newton, a posthumous child born with no father on Christmas Day, 1642, was the last wonder-child to whom the Magi could do sincere and appropriate homage."

"Says Seneca, some Body will demonstrate, which way Comets wander, why they go so far from the rest of the Celestial Bodies, how big, & what sort of Bodies they are, which had he been Contemporary with Sir Isaac he might have seen this Prophecy of his fulfill'd by that wonder of his Age."

— From a letter from Humphrey Newton to John Conduitt

Was Newton a Failure?

Newton was arguably the first, and possibly the greatest of all scientists. His discoveries and method transformed the nature and practice of learning, facilitating the modern world to such a degree that he has a good claim to be the most influential thinker who ever lived. Despite all this he famously described himself as "only like a boy playing on the sea shore"—was this simply modesty, or must Newton be accounted, by his own lights, a failure?

Newton's quest to decode the books of nature and scripture, to restore the *prisca sapientia* and the *prisca theologia*, must be understood in the context of his era. The old certainties that had governed the twin worlds of philosophy and theology for centuries were crumbling under assaults from every side.

The Crisis of Skepticism

Under the Medieval dispensation, knowledge of the natural and spiritual world was certain because it came from God, via Aristotle, the Bible, and the Church. Aristotle was the ultimate source of authority in matters natural and the Bible was the ultimate authority in matters spiritual; the Church used its authority to dictate interpretations of both. But this era of certainty had given way to a new era of skepticism; an era of doubting authority and challenging it.

In the world of natural philosophy, the new learning was challenging the scholastic system based on Aristotle. New approaches, like the mechanistic philosophy of Descartes, seemed to suggest that God might be unnecessary for the functioning of the universe. In the world of theology, the Reformation had challenged and overthrown the authority of the Church. A confusion of new sects and interpretations had been thrown up, nations had been riven by war and dissent. There was a crisis of skepticism, articulated by Descartes in his thought experiment about the "evil genius," in which he imagined a demon that controlled all the sensory input to his brain, presenting an illusion as reality. It would be impossible for him to know the difference—indeed, how could anyone be certain what the truth was?

Savior of the Human Race?

Newton wished to come to the rescue, "to save humanity from scepticism and usher in a new millennium," in the words of Betty Jo Teeter Dobbs. He believed he could succeed where others had failed. Descartes had believed that he could reassert certainty and solve the crisis of

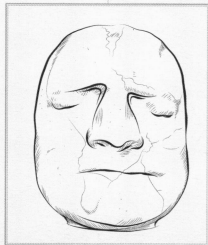

Newton's striking death mask, taken by the celebrated sculptor Louis François Roubiliac, now belongs to the Royal Society.

skepticism through mathematics; his contemporary, the Scottish minister John Dury, believed that the interpretation of Biblical philosophy was the route to truth. Where Newton was truly unique was in his refusal to limit himself to one approach, his courage to pursue every possible path. "Because his goal was a Truth that encompassed not only the 'mathematical principles of natural philosophy' but divinity as well," explains Dobbs, "Newton's balancing procedure included also the knowledge he had garnered from theology, revelation, alchemy, history, and the wise ancients." Through this holistic approach Newton was able to arrive at his great breakthroughs.

Fragments of the Whole

But Newton's ultimate goal eluded him. The "system of the world" he achieved was partial, unfinished. He had hoped to unify not only the macro- and microscopic levels of the natural world, with a theory that unified both atomic and celestial forces, but to unite the natural and supernatural worlds. He desired to bridge the physical and metaphysical with a unified theory that would bring under law all the realms of knowledge: natural philosophy, theology, and history.

Toward the end of his life he wrote: "I seem to have been only like a boy playing on the seashore, and diverting myself in now and then finding a smoother pebble or a prettier shell than ordinary, whilst the great ocean of truth lay all undiscovered before me." Typically this is interpreted as an expression of modesty, of humility in the face of his towering achievements, and at the same time a clarion call to subsequent generations of science to continue his labors. But in truth this was a lament, not a homily. Newton believed it had been his destiny to cross the ocean of truth and recover the *prisca sapientia*, yet he had brought back only fragments of the whole.

Newton dreamed of unifying microscopic and macroscopic forces in a unified theory that would also encompass the spiritual realm.

"To explain all nature is too difficult a task for any one man or even for any one age. Tis much better to do a little with certainty & leave the rest for others that come after you."

"GOD SAID 'LET NEWTON BE' AND ALL WAS LIGHT."

Sir Isaac Newton

1642–1727

Bibliography and References

The best place to read Newton's own notebooks, alchemical and theological papers and much other material relating to him is online at the Newton Project: www.newtonproject.sussex.ac.uk

Cohen, I.B. and Smith, G.E. (eds.) *The Cambridge Companion to Newton*, Cambridge University Press, 2002

Dobbs, B.J.T. *The Foundations of Newton's Alchemy, or "The Hunting of the Greene Lyon,"* Cambridge University Press, 1975

_____. *The Janus Faces of Genius: The Role of Alchemy in Newton's Thought*, Cambridge University Press, 1991

Edleston, J. (ed.) *Correspondence of Sir Isaac Newton and Professor Cotes*, John W. Parker, 1850

Fauvel, J. Flood, R., Shortland, M., and Wilson, R. (eds.) *Let Newton Be!* Oxford University Press, 1988

French, P.J. *John Dee: The World of an Elizabethan Magus*, Routledge and Kegan Paul, 1972

Gjertsen, D. *The Newton Handbook*, Routledge & Kegan Paul, 1986

Gleick, J. *Isaac Newton*, Fourth Estate, 2003

Hall, A.R. *Philosophers at War: The Quarrel between Newton and Leibniz*, Cambridge University Press, 1980

Harkness, D.E. *John Dee's Conversations with Angels: Cabala, Alchemy, and the End of Nature*, Cambridge University Press, 1999

Henry, J. *Knowledge is Power: How Magic, the Government and an Apocalyptic Vision inspired Francis Bacon to Create Modern Science*, Icon Books, 2002

Iliffe, R. *A Very Short Introduction to Isaac Newton*, Oxford University Press, 2007

Mandlebrote, S. *Footprints of the Lion: Isaac Newton at Work*, Cambridge University Library, 2001

Manuel, F. *A Portrait of Isaac Newton*, Harvard University Press, 1968

Maunder, E.W. "The Royal Observatory Greenwich: A glance at its history and work"; http://atschool.eduweb.co.uk/bookman/library/ROG/INDEX.HTM, accessed December 2008

Newton, I. *Opticks*, Prometheus Books, 2003

_____. *Principia, The Mathematical Principles of Natural Philosophy*, translated by Motte, A., revised by Cajori, F., University of California Press, 1962

Palter, Rt. *The Annus Mirabilis of Sir Isaac Newton 1666–1966*, MIT Press, 1970

Pickover, C.A. *Strange Brains and Genius*, Plenum Press, 1998

Pourciau, B. "Reading the Master: Newton and the Birth of Celestial Mechanics," *American Mathematical Monthly*, January 1997

Purkiss, D. *The English Civil War: A People's History*, Harper Perennial, 2007

Sabra, A.I. *Theories of Light from Descartes to Newton*, Cambridge University Press, 1981

Stukeley, W. *Memoirs of Sir Isaac Newton's Life*, 1752, Taylor & Francis, 1936

Sullivan, J.W.N. *Isaac Newton 1642–1727*, Macmillan and Co., 1938

Tomalin, C. *Samuel Pepys: The Unequalled Self*, Penguin, 2003

Turnbull, H.W., Scott, J.F., Hall, A.R., and Tilling, L. (eds.) *The Correspondence of Isaac Newton*, Seven Volumes, Cambridge University Press, 1959–77

Webster, C. *From Paracelsus to Newton: Magic and the Making of Modern Science*, Cambridge University Press, 1982

Westfall, R.S. *Never at Rest: A Biography of Isaac Newton*, Cambridge University Press, 1980

White, M. *Isaac Newton: The Last Sorcerer*, Fourth Estate, 1998

Index

Credits

All original artwork by Rob
 Brandt © Quid Publishing.
(PD = public domain images)
Other images credited
as follows:

Page 3 left reproduced
 with permission from
 www.shinyshack.com
Page 3 right PD
Page 5 Library of Congress
 Prints and Photographs
 Division
Page 7 PD
Page 9 Library of Congress
 Prints and Photographs
 Division
Page 14 PD
Page 15 PD
Page 18 PD
Page 29 Library of Congress
 Prints and Photographs
 Division
Page 31 © Bettmann/
 CORBIS
Page 33 © Bettmann/
 CORBIS
Page 34 © Bettmann/
 CORBIS
Page 37 right PD
Page 40 © Dreamstime

Page 43 top PD
Page 43 bottom PD
Page 45 Library of Congress
 Prints and Photographs
 Division
Page 46 PD
Page 50 © Bettmann/
 CORBIS
Page 52 PD
Page 53 PD
Page 55 © Hulton/CORBIS
Page 57 © Bettmann/
 CORBIS
Page 59 © Bettmann/
 CORBIS
Page 60 © Dreamstime
Page 61 © Bettmann/
 CORBIS
Page 62 Library of Congress
 Prints and Photographs
 Division
Page 65 PD
Page 66 PD
Page 67 left PD
Page 67 right PD
Page 68 PD
Page 70 PD
Page 71 © Bettmann/
 CORBIS
Page 73 Library of Congress
 Prints and Photographs
 Division
Page 74 PD
Page 75 © Bettmann/
 CORBIS
Page 78 PD

Page 79 top © Dreamstime
Page 81 top © Bettmann/
 CORBIS
Page 83 © Mary Evans
 Picture Library
Page 85 PD
Page 88 NASA
Page 89 © Bettmann/
 CORBIS
Page 91 Library of Congress
 Prints and Photographs
 Division
Page 96 © Bettmann/
 CORBIS
Page 97 © Bettmann/
 CORBIS
Page 98 PD
Page 99 PD
Page 100 PD
Page 101 © iStockphoto
Page 103 top PD
Page 103 center PD
Page 103 bottom PD
Page 104 PD
Page 106 PD
Page 107 top PD
Page 107 bottom PD
Page 109 Library of Congress
 Prints and Photographs
 Division
Page 110 PD
Page 111 © Bettmann/
 CORBIS
Page 112 PD
Page 113 PD
Page 115 © Bettmann/
 CORBIS

Page 117 PD
Page 119 © Bettmann/
 CORBIS
Page 121 PD
Page 125 top PD
Page 125 bottom PD
Page 127 © Getty Images
Page 128 PD
Page 130 © Bettmann/
 CORBIS
Page 131 NASA
Page 133 © Bettmann/
 CORBIS
Page 134 left PD
Page 134 right PD
Page 135 © Getty Images
Page 139 Library of Congress
 Prints and Photographs
 Division
Page 140 PD
Page 141 PD
Page 143 PD
Page 144 PD
Page 145 © Hutton/CORBIS
Page 146 © Bettmann/
 CORBIS
Page 149 © Bettmann/
 CORBIS
Page 150 PD
Page 151 PD
Page 152 PD
Page 153 left © Bettmann/
 CORBIS
Page 154 Library of Congress
 Prints and Photographs
 Division